Write on Target:

Preparing Young Writers to Succeed on State Writing Achievement Tests

Write on Target:

Preparing Young Writers to Succeed on State Writing Achievement Tests

Tommy Thomason

Carol York

Christopher-Gordon Publishers, Inc.
Norwood, Massachusetts

Credits

Every effort has been made to contact copyright holders for permission to reproduce borrowed material where necessary. We apologize for any oversights and will be happy to rectify them in future printings.

Narrative and expository writing prompts are included in this book with permission of the Florida Writing Assessment Program, Florida Department of Education, Tallahassee, Florida.

Student work used by permission of parents or legal guardians.

The "Kid Friendly Rubric" by Paulette Wasserstein from the CDE webpage is used with permission of the Colorado Department of Education.

The Bill Harp Professional Teacher's Library
An Imprint of
Christopher-Gordon Publishers, Inc.
1502 Providence Highway, Suite 12
Norwood, MA 02062
(800) 934-8322

Printed in the United States of America

10 9 8 7 6 5 4 3   05 04 03 02 01

Library of Congress Catalogue Card Number: 99-74261
ISBN: 0-926842-98-6

Contents

FOREWORD VII
Seeing the Possibilities
Michael R. Sampson, Ph.D.

FEREMENTATION IX
Brod Bagert

INTRODUCTION XI
Making Lemonade: Developing Successful Writers and Successful Test-Takers

WORKSHOP 1 1
Putting the Puzzle Together: Building a Writer-Friendly Classroom
    Encourage Risk-Taking 3
    Model the Writing Process 3
    Marinate Young Writers in Great Literature 6
    Write On: Provide Time to Write 7
    Explore the Composing Techniques of Authors: Using Literature
        as a Writing Model 9
    Conference Young Authors 10
    Teach Skills Through Writing 11
    Publish Student Writing 12
    Putting the Puzzle Together 13
    References 14

WORKSHOP 2 15
Building Fluency: Creating Confident Test-Takers

WORKSHOP 3 21
What is good writing anyway? Using Children's Literature to Teach Writing

WORKSHOP 4 27
Using Test Rubrics to Teach Writing
    What's a Rubric? 28

WORKSHOP 5 35
Teaching Narrative and Expository Writing
    Teaching Narrative Writing 36
    Teaching Expository Writing 40
    Notes 43
    References 43

WORKSHOP 6 .... **45**
More Than Just Elaboration: Creating Experiences for Readers
    Reference 49

WORKSHOP 7 .... **51**
A Potpourri of Writing Strategies: Adding Variety to Your Writing Workshop
    Experience Writing from Different Perspectives 52
    Teach the Skills of Writing 53
    Share Poetry Every Day 55
    And More 55
    References 57

WORKSHOP 8 .... **59**
Getting Ready for the Test: Preparing Parents, Students, and School
    Preparing Parents to Understand the Test 59
    Preparing Students to Take the Test 61
    Preparing the School to Support the Test 63

WORKSHOP 9 .... **65**
Frequently Asked Questions: Issues and Answers on Writing and Testing

AND SOME FINAL THOUGHTS **69**
Writers and Writing Tests: The Bottom Line

APPENDIX **71**
States Use Various Approaches to Assess Writing
Scott Beasley
    State Writing Assessments Grades 1–8 72
    Notes 75
    References 75

AUTHOR INDEX **77**

SUBJECT INDEX **78**

ABOUT THE AUTHORS **79**

FOREWORD

Seeing the Possibilities

Michael R. Sampson, Ph.D.

As we begin the 21st century, communication becomes the educational standard by which society will judge our students. And of all the communication skills, writing is perhaps the most visible and, sadly enough, the most judged and criticized language art.

Even with the push to improve writing at the end of the 20th century, students' ability to communicate clearly via writing did not increase—it decreased. The culprit? Some blame our response to state-mandated writing achievement tests.

In response to these mandates, teachers were sometimes side-tracked from the real purposes of writing, and the quality of student writing declined. But hope is on the way.

Write on Target recognizes the political reality of state writing assessments. But rather than respond through criticism, the book takes the positive approach of sharing techniques and strategies that develop not only extraordinary writers, but also writers who can display their mastery of the writing craft on state tests.

The authors are indeed qualified to speak to this issue. Tommy Thomason is a veteran writer and writing coach, and Carol York is an experienced teacher, administrator, and authority on writing assessment. I'm excited about this new, unique book. It takes a posi-

Michael Sampson is a professor of education at Texas A&M University–Commerce. He is the author of many scholarly articles, as well as professional books for teachers and curriculum for the classroom. He has also written picture books for children, including *The Football That Won* and *Star of the Circus*. He has also co-authored several picture books with Bill Martin Jr.

tive look at the classroom and the role of the classroom teacher to evoke better writing instruction through research-proven methods. It's a book that will help writing teachers prepare students to shift into the appropriate writing genre as they encounter different writing tasks. But most of all, it's a book that brings encouragement and hope to teachers and students alike.

An American statesman once said, "Some men see things as they are and ask, 'Why?' I see things as they could be and ask, Why not?" Tommy Thomason and Carol York have gazed upon the confused world of writing instruction and have seen possibilities—not obstacles. They see classrooms where writers write with confidence, connect with audiences, and develop the craft of writing by writing.

And their challenge to the writing teacher is, "Why not?"

Fermentation

By Brod Bagert

Authors' Note: Writing achievement tests have generated much controversy among educators during the last two decades. The premise of Write on Target *is that when teachers approach writing as an authentic classroom activity, students can grow as writers and still score well on the state test. Other voices in education look at the potentially damaging effects of the tests. Here poet Brod Bagert creates a classroom scenario that shows both the potential downside of writing tests and one teacher's desire to ensure a child's future as a writer.*

My first experience
with the *new* writing assessment
And this was the expository prompt:
　　Every one has favorite after-school activities.
　　Before you begin writing, think about one of your favorite after-
　　school activities.
　　Now explain why you like your after-school activities. You have
　　45 minutes. Now write.
So Matthew Ertling,
My star student,
Answered by writing a poem:

Brod Bagert writes poetry for adults and poetry for children to perform. His children's poetry books include *Let Me Be the Boss, Elephant Games, Chicken Socks,* and *The Gooch Machine.*

Crushed
By Matthew Ertling

Writing about this prompt is a chore.
I do it because you make me.
But it makes me feel ridiculous!
Oh how could you forsake me?

I remember how in third grade
The words I wrote were a song.
But my fourth-grade words are silent
and my writing feels all wrong.

The pages once poured from my heart
and my sentences soared like birds,
But now you give me prompts
And I paste together words.

I have written these words to please you,
But on this you can depend,
Though I give you what you want today,
I may never write again.

I read it . . .
Thought about it . . .
And responded to Matthew with a poem of my own:

A Promise
By Mrs. Cox

Please, try to understand,
I do what I have to,
For the very press that crushed your heart
Is crushing my heart too.

But I promise, I will find a way
For your sake and for mine,
Somehow I'll find a way to turn
Our crushed hearts into wine.

©Brod Bagert 1999

INTRODUCTION

Making Lemonade: Developing Successful Writers and Successful Test-Takers

❖ ❖ ❖ ❖ ❖ ❖ ❖

It happens to some of our most promising young writers.

When Tamika's second grade teacher asked her what she wanted to be when she grew up, the 8-year-old answered confidently.

"I'm going to be a writer," she said. "I've already published several books, you know."

Tamika was hooked on writing in first grade, where her teacher encouraged her to write about what she knew. That love of writing grew in the second and third grades. By the end of the third grade she was writing her own chapter books and experimenting with poetry.

But by the time she reached the fifth grade, Tamika no longer wanted to be a writer. She told her mother that writing was boring. When her teacher told the class to get out their journals, Tamika's voice joined in whining, "Do we have to?"

What happened to this promising young writer?

Fourth grade.

A year spent preparing for her state writing achievement test. A year that turned writing from a joyful challenge into a joyless chore.

❖ ❖ ❖ ❖ ❖ ❖ ❖

And it happens to teachers, too.

Jana arrived for her first year of teaching in September fresh-faced and optimistic, ready for her new class of fourth graders.

She had graduated from one of her state's top teacher-education programs, so Jana wasn't naive about the challenges awaiting her. But what she hadn't given much thought to was the one fact of fourth-grade life that dominated the conversation—and seemed to drive the curriculum—of her new colleagues: the state writing achievement test.

Other fourth grade teachers warned Jana that no matter what she might hear about the district's commitment to a balanced literacy program, the bottom-line reality was that her job security ultimately rested on the scores of her class on the state's test, which consisted of a writing prompt to provide either a story starter for a narrative or a topic for a persuasive essay.

Jana did not look forward to the pressure to perform that would be placed on her students. But she was most apprehensive about the recommendations her colleagues gave her for assuring the success of her student writers.

"I know you want to do all that writing process stuff," one older colleague advised her, "and that might work well in first or second or even third grade. A process approach will probably help your students feel good about themselves as writers, but it won't develop the skills they need to pass the test."

Another colleague told her that she would have to "teach to the test" until it was administered in March.

Still another lamented what she called the "sad dropoff" of student interest in writing during fourth grade: "Lots of students come to us from writing classrooms where they are used to choosing most of their topics and publishing their work. Unfortunately, we've got to spend time preparing for the test, and publication is a luxury we just don't have time for."

The way Jana saw it, she had two choices: Sacrifice the long-term writing development of her fourth graders by teaching to the test and thereby assuring that her students would make acceptable scores, or run her writer's workshop as she had planned and risk poor scores.

The new teacher was heartbroken. It seemed she would have to sacrifice all of her dreams of a process-oriented writing classroom to the state-mandated test and hope she could salvage some of her writing philosophy during the two months of school that remained after the test was given.

She took little comfort in the knowledge that she was only one of thousands of American teachers facing this dilemma—and coming up with answers both they and their young writers found unsatisfying.

In Florida, they call it Florida Writes. In New York, it's the Pupil Evaluation Program. And in Hawaii, students take the Hawaii Writing Assessment.

Shakespeare assured us that a rose by any other name would smell as sweet. Classroom teachers throughout the United States claim that writing achievement tests—no matter what they are called—can disrupt their entire year and sometimes turn children against writing.

If you're looking for an argument against the validity of writing achievement tests, you won't find it here. Lots of other books deal with the issue of whether or not mandated tests really measure the competencies they have been designed to assess.[1] But writing achievement tests are a fact of school life, so this book approaches writing tests in the spirit of an old piece of folk wisdom: *If you have a lemon, make lemonade.*

In other words, how can we help students to write confidently, to see themselves as writers, to develop the skills writers need, to find audiences for their words . . . and at the same time to succeed on the state writing achievement test? Is it really possible to have your cake and eat it, too?

The answer is yes. The following pages will guide you through nine workshops designed to share strategies for success on writing tests. The workshops will give you practical ideas you can implement in your classroom to set the stage for test success without compromising your children's growth as writers.

Note

[1]   For an excellent discussion of the history of writing achievement tests in American Schools and how they reflect current educational philosophy, see P. LaCoste, *Coming to Terms: An Analysis of Large-Scale Writing Assessment in History, Theory, and Practice.* Ph.D. dissertation. Milwaukee: The University of Wisconsin–Milwaukee, 1997.

WORKSHOP 1

Putting the Puzzle Together:
Building a Writer-Friendly Classroom

❖ ❖ ❖ ❖ ❖ ❖ ❖

There is one inescapable fact of writing instruction: You can't teach writing.

Football coaches understand this principle. They can teach the rules of football. They can demonstrate blocking and tackling. They can give their players opportunities to practice the principles they have just demonstrated on a blocking sled or on each other. They can diagram plays on the board. They can order uniforms and schedule games. But the coach doesn't play a single down. All he can do is to stand on the sideline and watch.

Writing teachers can model and demonstrate and teach principles, but teachers can't make students into good writers. What we can do is to create an environment that encourages writing and honors writing. We create an environment where writing is a normal part of every day—where we read the work of other writers and produce texts ourselves to entertain and inform audiences within our classroom and beyond.

Writing researcher Janet Emig (1982) put it this way: "Writing is predominantly learned rather than taught" (p. 2021).

Some teachers, in their zeal to improve test scores, set up the type of writing environment that stifles, rather than encourages, writing development. The strategies they adopt to improve test scores actually discourage their students' writing development.

How do you put together this writer-friendly environment, the classroom atmosphere that encourages writing and promotes children's interest in the skills and writing techniques we will teach? Look at it as though you were putting together a puzzle, with each piece being a necessary part of that learning environment. You may well be in uncharted waters here personally—most teachers say they were never part of such an environment during their own school careers. All the pieces must be in the puzzle for maximum effect. Some people put together complicated puzzles and show them proudly to friends, even frame them for display. But if you lose even a single piece of your puzzle, the effect is destroyed.

So let's look at how the puzzle pieces (see Figure 1.1) fit together to see what classroom teachers can do to provide a writer-friendly atmosphere for young authors.

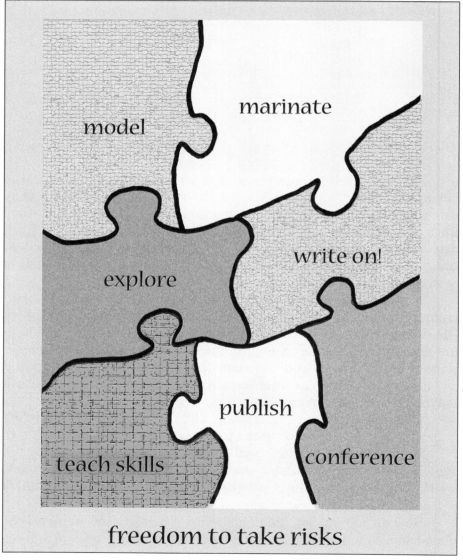

Figure 1.1 The writer-friendly classroom

Encourage Risk-Taking

Notice that this puzzle has a frame that holds it together: a workshop atmosphere where all writers feel free to take risks. What exactly is a workshop? Perhaps you took some classes in your university's art department as an undergraduate. In art history classes, you may remember the professor talking about Baroque art and the society and culture that fostered it. The professor probably also showed slides of Baroque painting and sculpture. You took notes, you observed, perhaps you even asked questions. But across the hall, another class was under way—a painting workshop. The professor might have given some instruction at the beginning, but soon each student was at an easel, working on his or her painting. The professor passed among students, offering advice and encouragement and asking questions. In art history, students were learning about paintings. In art workshop, students *were* painting.

In writing workshop, students write. They feel free to play with words because they know that everything will not be graded and that the teacher looks for opportunities to celebrate success. The atmosphere is warm and encouraging, and the teacher is herself a writer who shares her own works in progress.

Linda Crafton (1991) points out the necessity of establishing an environment where young writers can take chances:

> Playing it safe is a dead end when it comes to language and learning. Being able to try things out in a nonthreatening environment is the key to increasing language facility. To a great degree risk-taking is a trust issue. I know which peers will respond to my work in ways that help me focus on my message. . . . Likewise, I know which peers will be so critical that I feel like abandoning the effort. [Writing requires] so much rough-draft thinking that it's easy to feel vulnerable. (pp. 15–16)

And when are young writers more vulnerable than when taking a standardized writing achievement test? Students whose workshop environment has made them comfortable with risk-taking and comfortable with writing and unafraid of failure have a definite advantage when they sit down to respond to the state's writing prompt.

Model the Writing Process

Many veteran writing teachers claim that the most important thing they do both to teach writing and to build a writer-friendly classroom is to write with their children. These teachers typically spend a few minutes of every writing workshop modeling what writers do: They write. A Texas teacher who attended a workshop conducted by one of the authors later wrote this letter:

> For the first time ever, I'm writing with my fifth graders this year. As I told you at the workshop, I never had good writing experiences myself in school, so this was a big step for me. But I explained the concept of a workshop to my students, and told them that we would be writing for about 45 minutes a day, and that for about half that time, I would be writing with them. I told them I hoped to see as much improvement in my own writing this year as I saw in theirs. I'll never forget the day I shared my first piece with them, during our first week of writing workshop. I was as nervous as if I had been giving a speech to a group of adults. But they were genuinely interested and asked lots of questions. I told them how some of those questions represented information I should have put in my piece, and that I would re-write tomorrow. I revised my piece the next day and shared it again. I think my class learned more about revision during those two days than during any week of lessons on revision I used to teach.
>
> I remember that quote you used from Donald Graves, that to teach writing well a teacher has to be willing to dance naked before her class. I thought it was funny at the time, but that's exactly how I felt at first. I now see that when I began to write was when students really saw how writing works and saw an adult who thought writing was important enough to do it herself. If I could change one thing about my first eight years in the classroom, I would start writing with my class from day one.

That teacher's endorsement of modeling the writing process came after only four months of writing with her students. Tom Romano (1987), a veteran teacher and writing authority, explained why the teacher's writing example has such a powerful effect on students:

> The sharing of my messes, my writing under construction, had a salutary effect on classroom atmosphere. I came to look upon my students differently. From a judge ready to pronounce sentence I metamorphosed into an advocate of student writers, a helper and fellow crafter. And their view of me changed. They began to perceive me as one who wrote and knew about

writing, not merely as someone who was a stickler for standard usage and punctuation and who always had in mind an ideal way of writing something. The teacher, they saw, wrestled with the same problems they did—a comforting fact for a learner. (p. 42)

When teachers share both their writing processes and their writing products with their students, they do the one thing non-writers need most: They *demystify* writing. We all tend to mystify skills—we see them as something someone else can do, but not us. Even when we are given instruction on how to do them ourselves, they seem somehow inaccessible.

That's because in the classroom we tend to share two facets of writing. First, completed products. We show students examples of good writing, from trade books to well-written samples of student work. We also give them instructions on how to produce a product like the one they have read. What we *don't* show is the process, how to begin with an idea and apply those principles of good writing to produce a well-written product.

Let's say you visit an art museum to see a Van Gogh exhibit. You stand in front of the master's works, impressed with his artistry. As you leave the museum, you are still talking about Van Gogh's ability as an artist, but you do not leave with a desire to take up painting or a belief that you, too, could produce such visual beauty.

But perhaps you go home and turn on your TV. Channel-surfing, you come across PBS's *The Joy of Painting,* where you see painter Bob Ross standing before a blank canvas, telling you that you can produce a picture like the one he is about to paint. You're incredulous, but you watch as he takes his brush and begins to paint. He shows a few simple brushstrokes that produce a tree. You watch as a green hillside emerges from the canvas and you listen as Ross explains and demonstrates the simplicity of what he is doing. You think to yourself, I could do that.

What's the difference between your experience at the museum and your experience with Bob Ross? At the museum, you saw Van Gogh's products and you were awed, but you never even considered the possibility that you might produce such a product. But when you saw Ross's process, painting was *demystified.* You saw how he did it. You saw an artist turn a blank canvas into a painting. Ross demonstrated and explained. And as you watched, you began to see how you, too, could paint a picture. The same thing happens to your students when you demystify the process by writing with them.

Marinate Young Writers in Great Literature

When you find a class that enjoys writing, you also typically find a teacher who reads aloud every day to his or her students. You find a classroom that's littered with literacy—it's full of trade books and student-authored books. Charts hang from every available protrusion on the walls, sometimes even from the ceiling. Students have time to read, to sing, to perform poetry and to dramatize books. Children often choose what they are to read.

Good writing teachers marinate their students in beautiful language. Reading to students isn't a waste of valuable instructional time—it's a necessary step in the development of a young writer. Computer programmers have understood this for years. Their acronym GIGO (garbage in, garbage out) reminds them that their products are results of their processes, that output problems are the result of input problems. One of the best ways to increase sentence fluency, vocabulary, and "story sense," as well as give your students ideas for writing and models to follow, is to expose them to good writing so they can unconsciously assimilate aspects of the literature they hear and read. Recognizing that many students live in a literary wasteland, Mem Fox (1993) reminds us that teachers need to "water the desert so the writing will bloom." (p. 67)

Author/teacher Bill Martin Jr. (1990) has a writer's understanding of the value of immersing students in the sounds of language:

> Reading aloud to children sensitizes them to patterns of words that repeat over and over in our language; it skyrockets individual words into a burst of awareness that lasts a lifetime. . . .
>
> Each of us has a linguistic storehouse into which we deposit patterns for stories and poems and sentences and words. These patterns enter the memory through the ear and remain available, ready to be cued into action, throughout the whole of a lifetime, providing advance information that is valuable for reading, writing, speaking, listening, and thinking. (pp. 39–40)

Kathy Robinson, a writing specialist who works in all fourth grade classes at Cypress Creek Elementary in Ruskin, Florida, faces a real challenge in marinating her students in the language of children's literature. Her school has a 92 percent mobility rate. More than half are enrolled in a program for students with limited English proficiency and the poverty level among students' families is 83 percent. Her students frequently have little exposure to books at home before they come to her class, but Kathy knows that exposure is critical if her fourth graders are to build a literary "data bank" that will serve them well in their Florida Writes test.

So Kathy sends home bookbags with several students each week. The bags include cassette tapes, videotapes, books, activities the whole family can participate in, and instructions for either an essay the student will write during the week or writing-related activities like writing a poem, responding to literature, completing a graphic organizer or locating 10 nouns or verbs on a certain topic from their reading. The contents of the bookbag are oriented around the theme of the assigned essay, and the bookbag also contains activities to involve young authors and their families, such as:

- information about how to write the essay in different formats, such as a fold-out, an accordion, or a flip-book;
- writing supplies, such as scented markers, tape, a stapler, and erasers;
- all levels of books, so any reader in the family can find something appropriate (Kathy avoids embarrassment over sending some very easy readers by telling children that they can read these to their younger brothers and sisters).

Each bag contains a journal, and family members of the student are encouraged to write about the activities they complete together. She gives the children a treat for returning the bag intact and ready for the next family.

Kathy uses the bookbag and other strategies similar to the ones discussed in this book. And it's definitely paying off—last year 100 percent of Cypress Creek fourth graders passed the Florida Writes expository writing test and only nine failed the narrative test, a dramatic improvement over the previous year. Kathy says she is sold on the bookbag idea because the bookbags excite children about writing and because they help to get the patterns and vocabulary and sounds of good writing into students' minds and hearts.

Write On: Provide Time to Write

The most obvious shortcoming of "teaching to the (writing achievement) test" is that students spend so much time studying *about* writing and test-taking, time that detracts from the only thing that ultimately builds writers: writing itself.

If your teen-ager has even taken driver's education, you know that student drivers study driving manuals and spend some classtime learning the rules of the road. But ultimately, adolescents don't learn to drive from a book or a class. There's only one way, only one place to learn to drive—behind the wheel of a car. If your teen is a poor driver, you know that the answer is not to re-read the manual or take refresher courses. Poor drivers need to spend time learning behind the wheel, with an experienced driver in the passenger's seat to answer questions, give suggestions, even occasionally to slide into the driver's seat for a demonstration.

The same goes for young writers. These writers, marinated in beautiful language in the classroom, now must have an opportunity to write themselves in a workshop atmosphere. When writing becomes a daily activity, young writers begin to look at their lives in a different way. They begin to see the writing topics that surround them because they know that sometime during the school day they will sit down to write. One of the greatest writing myths is that one reason non-writers avoid writing is because they have nothing to say. If they had something to say, the reasoning goes, they would write. The truth is just the opposite: If they would write, they would have something to say. Donald Graves (1994) points out that when children write every day, they think more often of the act of writing, entering into "a constant state of composition" (p. 104).

Workshop 2 examines the idea of *writing fluency* as one of the primary determinants of success on writing achievement tests. And fluency—comfort with the writing process—can be achieved only through spending time writing. Not talking about writing. Not teaching about writing. Not preparing to write. Not studying lessons on writing. Those are important, but nothing substitutes for writing itself. Professional writers understand that. Susan Shaughnessy (1993) wrote about an attitude toward writing that can make as much difference in the classroom as it does in the lives of writing professionals:

> The word *amateur* is from the French, "one who loves." There is nothing wrong with loving to write. But loving to write is not enough. Writers are those who write. They write when they are depressed; when they are elated; when they are in love; when they are in despair; when they need dental work, and when they don't. They write because they write. (p. 6)

Balanced classroom writing programs offer many opportunities to write in different settings, including the following.

- In writing workshop students select their topics and write in a workshop setting that includes conferencing, editing, revision, and publication.

- Journal writing gives students an opportunity to write personal, reflective pieces on a regular basis. Most of this writing is not read by the teacher unless students write in interactive journals that offer teachers an opportunity to respond and even carry on written dialogues with students.

- Instructional writing follows craft lessons. Teachers share a lesson on, say, visual writing or the use of strong verbs and then give students practice in using that skill or concept. The writing may be a dialogue written just to practice recording and punctuating oral conversation in print. It may be describing an object in the classroom to develop the ability to use details to paint visual pictures with words. That practice may even include worksheets giving students the opportunity to apply the skill just discussed. Some teachers condemn these worksheet-type exercises as meaningless skill drills, purely decontextualized learning. And that would be true if authentic writing were not going on every day in the classroom. But if students are writing daily in a variety of contexts, they will take the skills they practice and use them in their writing. Of course, it is up to the teacher to point out examples in literature of authors' use of that same writing technique and to remind students of their opportunity to use the technique in appropriate places during conferencing.

- Writing across the curriculum gives students opportunities to write in the content areas. Learning logs, reports, informational books written for younger classes and other expository-type texts not only give students additional writing practice, they also facilitate learning because writing about a topic requires a deeper level of understanding.

Explore the Composing Techniques of Authors: Using Literature as a Writing Model

When students read every day, are read to every day, and write every day, teachers can make the obvious connection between reading and writing by initiating students into the secret world of authors. Those who watch magicians are mystified by card tricks and levitation and bunnies that appear in top hats. But those who actually study magic and begin to perform magic can be initiated into the art of the magician. They can begin to learn how the magician performs the illusions.

Those who only read can be caught up in the art of a master storyteller. But those who also write every day can begin to study the storyteller's art to see *how* he or she involves the reader in the story.

Across the nation, one of the favorite books of fourth graders is Jerry Spinelli's *Maniac McGhee*. Students involved in that book will find it hard to put down. But fourth graders who have read *Maniac McGhee* can also begin to look at the storyteller's craft. Why is it such a good book? In a mini-lesson, teachers point out Spinelli's masterful use of dialogue. They copy a few pages of that dialogue for students to study. They look at other examples of effective dialogue in books they enjoy by Beverly Cleary or Lois Lowry or Gary Paulsen. They study the punctuation of dialogue and see how writers use punctuation to show a change of speaker. Then they use what they have learned as they introduce dialogue into their own pieces.

Some of the nation's most effective writing teachers begin with a book children already love, perhaps a book that has already inspired an art activity or even a classroom choral reading. They isolate a characteristic of good writing from that book and build a mini-lesson around it, showing students how effective use of that technique can enhance their enjoyment of a story and how they can use the same techniques professional writers employ. Identifying the composing techniques of authors helps to demystify writing, because it shows young writers how to transfer what they have learned into their own work. Workshop 3 examines ways you can use the books children already love to teach the principles of writing that will be so valuable when they write for an audience or take a state writing test.

Conference Young Authors

Many teachers say the most effective thing they do as a writing teacher is to conference their young authors. The best conferences are typically short, from under a minute to three or four minutes at the most, offering teacher and student an opportunity to interact briefly about a work in process.

The primary goal of a conference is always to show students how to "think like a writer." In some conferences, a teacher will praise a student for a well-crafted lead or an effective descriptive paragraph, telling the writer specifically what he or she did well and how that demonstrates growth as a writer. In other conferences, the teacher gives the student an opportunity to talk briefly about writing problems or where he or she is going with the piece at hand. Teachers ask young writers to paraphrase what they have written, to find a sentence or two they like especially and read it, to share where they are going or what they plan to do next with the piece. The most effective conferences are probably when the teacher just reacts as a reader to the piece, asking for more information or commenting on the topic, not on the effectiveness of the piece of writing.

Carole Avery (1993) says her conference interactions with students are guided by a simple goal:

> In . . . short, frequent conferences with children, my goal is to help the writer. So I respond to the writer, not the writing, and trust that if I help the writer, the writing will come. (p. 149)

Conferencing is so effective for intermediates because it lets them think out loud about what they have written. Through the type of questions any interested reader would ask, teachers can help young writers focus on areas where they have left questions unanswered. Instead of writing a marginal comment like "Tell me more about this!" the teacher actually asks writers for more information. Young writers talk about what was in their mind as they wrote—what "pictures" were in their heads. It is much easier then for authors to write down what they just heard themselves say out loud.

If you have questions about how to implement conferencing in your classroom, you might want to read a practical, step-by-step book on how to get started, *Writer to Writer: How to Conference Young Authors* (1998), written by one of the co-authors of this book.

Teach Skills Through Writing

Perhaps the biggest myth in circulation about the process-oriented classroom is that children in these classes do not learn the skills associated with writing—especially grammar usage, spelling, and punctuation. The truth is actually just the opposite: Only students who write regularly really learn the conventions, because they learn them in the context of actually writing. Writers understand the real purposes of the conventions—as aids to readability. For example, they learn to use quotation marks correctly because they are writing narratives that use dialogue. Summarizing the research on teaching skills in the context of writing, Regie Routman (1996) wrote:

> For improving editing skills, it is most effective and efficient to teach only the grammatical concepts that are critically needed for editing writing, and to teach these concepts and their terms mostly through minilessons and writing conferences, particularly while helping students to edit their writing. (p. 201)

Teachers in writer-friendly classrooms never let young writers forget the reason to master grammar, spelling, and punctuation: to make writing more effective and easier for the reader with the minimum of distractions from non-standard usages. One Texas teacher prefaces almost every statement about grammar with the phrase "Writers use . . ." So if he talks about effective use of adverbs, he begins sentences with "Writers use adverbs to . . ." His young writers have many reminders that grammar is a tool that writers use, and the reason they study grammar is to become more effective writers. Journalist and writing coach Roy Peter Clark (1987) explains that this approach is the key to helping writers appreciate and really learn grammar:

> I learned to punctuate when I stopped asking "What's the rule here?" and began asking "How can I use this comma to make my meaning clear?" The difference is profound. Emphasis on the rule inhibits the writer; emphasis on the tool has the writer reaching to his workbench for something that will help him. (p. 137)

Countless research articles throughout the 20th century have documented what good writing teachers frequently feel instinctively: that first you help students to become writers, and then teach skills in the context of authorship and publication. One of the most influential of these articles, an NCTE report titled *Research in Written Composition* (R. Braddock et al., 1963), concludes with these often-quoted words:

> In view of the widespread agreement of research studies based upon many types of students and teachers, the conclusion can be stated in strong and unqualified terms: the teaching of formal grammar has a negligible, or, because it usually displaces some instruction and practice in actual composition, even a harmful effect on the improvement of writing. (pp. 37–38)

Publish Student Writing

No matter what else you may be doing in your classroom, you cannot say you have a truly writer-friendly atmosphere until students have opportunities to publish some of what they write. Writing without publishing is like cooking a gourmet meal and throwing it away. Combining ingredients in exactly the right proportions can be a challenge, and sautéing or baking until exactly the right moment can be a learning experience, but if you never eat the meal, the chef feels a sense of incompleteness. A chef-in-training might cook occasionally just for the practice, but even that practice is to perfect his or her art for eventual consumption. Like speech, writing is communication. We perfect our speech because we use it to communicate meaningfully with others. What is the motivation for writing unless we share it with an audience?

When students have an opportunity to publish, writing takes on a "real-world" flavor. And nothing sparks children's desire to write as much as the prospect of sharing their work with an audience.

When they think of publication, many teachers think of student-made books. But that's only the beginning. Other forms of publication include exchanging letters or e-mail with others outside the class; publishing a classroom newspaper; writing letters to the editors of outside publications; encouraging children to enter writing contests found in children's magazines; preparing books and anthologies for authors' teas and inviting parents and other relatives; compiling classroom poetry anthologies; setting poems to music; writing plays to present in class and videotape for later presentation in other classes; and writing curriculum-related books for younger classes, such as an ABC book on dinosaurs or insects or Thanksgiving to go along with a thematic unit.

Publication is the primary motivator of both editing and revision. Children who never get to publish their work also never have the opportunity to experience the best motivation to make it better by revising for enhanced meaning or cleaning up errors in grammar, spelling, and punctuation.

Putting the Puzzle Together

These are the pieces of the puzzle; put them together and you have a writer-friendly classroom, the type of classroom that grows successful test writers. The workshops that follow outline strategies that produce the types of writers who score well on state writing assessment tests. But just as you wouldn't buy a tropical plant and expect it to thrive in a Frost Belt climate, you can't expect these strategies to work if you don't transplant them into a writer-friendly classroom.

Before you go on, ask yourself these questions to see how well you have the various parts of the puzzle put together in your classroom:

1. Do your young writers—and you, too—feel free to take risks, to try new things in writing, to share works in progress, to ask for help?

2. Do you write with your class? Do they see you writing during part of their writing workshop time? Do you share your writing with them? Do you let them ask questions and make suggestions based on pieces you have shared? Do you ever revise your work and show them how and why you made changes?

3. Do you immerse your class in beautiful language? Do you read both prose and poetry to them regularly? Do they have time to read for pleasure in class? To select some of their own reading materials?

4. Do you give your students time to write every day? Is writing workshop a regular part of your classroom routine?

5. Do you use literature as a writing model? Do you take some of the children's classroom favorites and analyze the writing to see what techniques the writers have used to make their books effective?

6. Do you conference your young writers? Do you conduct short one-on-one conferences during writing workshop? Do you conduct editing conferences with students who are ready to move on to publication?

7. Do you study skills in the context of writing? Do you relate grammar study, for example, to the writing that your young authors are doing?

8. Do your students publish some of what they write? Do they read some of their writing in Author's Chair or some other form of whole-group or small-group sharing? Do your classroom bookshelves contain books written by your students?

If you answered *yes* to most of the questions above, you're ready to add some strategies that have proven helpful in classrooms around the United States in preparing young writers to excel on state writing achievement tests.

References

Avery, C. (1993) . . . *And with a light touch.* Portsmouth, NH: Heinemann.

Braddock, R., Lloyd-Jones, R., & Schoer, L. (1963) *Research in written composition.* Urbana, IL: National Council of Teachers of English.

Clark, R. P. (1987). *Free to write.* Portsmouth, NH: Heinemann.

Crafton, L. K. (1991). *Whole language: Getting started . . . moving forward.* Katonah, NY: Richard C. Owens Publishers.

Emig, J. (1982). "Writing, Composition, and Rhetoric." In *Encyclopedia of Educational Research,* 5th ed., Vol. 4. New York: Free Press.

Fox, M. (1993). *Radical reflections.* San Diego: Harcourt Brace.

Graves, D. (1994). *A fresh look at writing.* Portsmouth, NH: Heinemann.

Martin, B. (1990). "An Essay for Teachers," in *Sounds of laughter*, Bill Martin Sounds of Language series. Allen, TX: DLM.

Romano, T. (1987). *Clearing the way.* Portsmouth, NH: Heinemann.

Routman, R. (1996). *Literacy at the crossroads.* Portsmouth, NH: Heinemann.

Shaughnessy, S. (1994). *Walking on alligators: A book of meditations for writers.* San Francisco: HarperSanFrancisco.

Thomason, T. (1998) *Writer to writer: How to conference young authors.* Norwood, MA: Christopher-Gordon.

WORKSHOP 2

Building Fluency: Creating Confident Test-Takers

❖ ❖ ❖ ❖ ❖ ❖ ❖

Ask anyone who ever learned to drive a car with a standard transmission. They'll recount those days of grinding gears, watching the speedometer (often instead of the road) and thinking of the upcoming shift from second to third gear, reminding themselves to push the clutch all the way in—and of course, the abject fear of catching a red light at the top of a hill.

But if they have been driving a standard for very long, they'll tell you they never think of those concerns now. It's all second nature. They are sometimes not even aware that they are changing gears on the highway. What happened? How does driving a standard or cooking or delivering a speech or making love become second-nature? How do we go from looking at the activity with some discomfort to seeing it as a normal—even routine—part of life?

The key is found in one word: fluency. Dictionaries define it as speaking or writing easily, smoothly, or expressively.

Fluency is perhaps the most-overlooked key to success on writing achievement tests. In even the best scenarios, these tests represent a pressure-packed situation for young writers. They have to think quickly and write, with little opportunity to use some of the brainstorming strategies that are so much a part of a writer's workshop environment. There is no conferencing, no peer editing, little opportunity to revise, none of the writer's resources normally available as a matter of course when they compose. They write to a prompt they didn't choose and which they may not be interested in or have much to say about.

Who performs best in those situations? Fluent writers. That is, writers who write easily and smoothly. Writers who don't fear writing. Writers for whom the act of composing is as normal and natural as sitting down to eat lunch or read a book or play a game. Or to expand the driving analogy, who would do better in a race—an inexperienced driver who still got nervous in traffic or an experienced driver who was comfortable behind the wheel? The competition would pose a challenge for both drivers. But at least the experienced driver could concentrate on the race and not on the mechanics of driving.

The same is true for writers. Fluent writers will be more able to draw upon their creativity because they are just more comfortable with the act of writing.

The next logical question then is how do we build fluency? Luckily, the answer is simple. And it's the same answer you would give if someone asked how you create fluent—comfortable, at-ease—drivers. For drivers, you simply have to spend a lot of time behind the wheel, actually driving. For writers, you have to write. The Nike ads say it best: "Just do it."

The more students write, the more fluent they become and therefore better able to cope with the test.

What this *doesn't* mean is that all types of writing are equal, that any writing a student does will make him or her into a fluent writer.

Indeed, if fluency represents a comfort level with the act of writing, you can't achieve comfort in uncomfortable writing situations. The following factors have been shown to create comfortable writing environments for young writers:

Writing should be authentic.   In writing terminology, that just means *real*. Let's say we took children out to the playground and told them that being able to hit a round object with a stick was a valuable skill. Then, day after day, we instructed them on how to hit the object. We even threw the object so it would pass close to the children, to give them an opportunity to hit it. Occasionally we would assess their ability to hit the object. They would soon become bored with what they considered meaningless outdoor schoolwork. But let's say we defined the stick as a bat and the round object as a ball. Then we told them that hitting the ball with a bat was a way to get on base or advance runners who were already on base. And advancing runners on base was the way to win a game we called baseball. It completely changes our approach to hitting the round object. What we did, by adding the game, was to make the skill of hitting *authentic*. We can do the same thing with writing by treating it as meaningful communication, by giving students an opportunity to publish and share what they have written, by not treating writing constantly as an project to be assessed or even improved.

Children are natural storytellers, and wonderfully egocentric—they enjoy telling others about their pet and their toys and their team and their weekend and their ideas. And they enjoy writing when they understand that print is talk written down and that the first reason to write is to share yourself and your ideas with others. This sharing is so important and so fulfilling and so joyous that it becomes even more fulfilling when we learn certain writers' techniques for making our stories even more effective and compelling. That leads to our writing curriculum. Any baseball coach will tell you that a child is ready to accept coaching and ready to spend hours in baseball practice when he or she loves the game and desperately wants to play it better. Young writers will accept, and even seek, instruction when writing is important to them because they see it as an authentic activity.

Authentic writing should be an everyday activity.   Fluency is closely tied with habit, and habit comes from regular use. Writing teacher Nancie Atwell (1998) explained the importance of making writing a part of the classroom routine:

> Without at least three writing workshops a week (preferably four or five), it will be hard for kids to conceive topics, sustain projects of their own, and behave as writers.
>
> Regular, frequent time for writing also helps students write well. When they have sufficient time to consider and reconsider what they've written, they're more likely to achieve the clarity, logic, voice, conventionality, and grace of good writing. (p. 91)

You may be thinking that students writing during a test do not have time to "consider and reconsider what they've written" and thus achieve the writing quality Atwell speaks of. And that's true. But young writers—or even older writers—will never achieve those qualities on a timed test and under pressure until they have first achieved them in writer's workshop with the opportunity to draft, rewrite, conference, and revise. Young writers first gain confidence and skill by working in a workshop environment. When they begin to develop their skills as writers and become more confident and ready to take risks, they are better able to cope with the writing situation presented by the test.

Fluency occurs naturally when young writers catch their teacher's passion for writing.   A love for writing is more caught than it is taught, and when teachers write with their students and share their works in progress and show obvious excitement about their own writing development, those students come to value writing more.

The authors have interviewed great writing teachers throughout the nation, teachers whose children have posted outstanding scores on state writing achievement tests. Invariably, these young authors were already fluent writers when they took the test. And invariably, their teachers were also writers. Many children know that their teachers place real priority on standardized tests. They hear the admonitions every day. They see the practice sheets for the tests. The walls are adorned with bulletin boards admonishing them to take the test seriously, to do their best work, even to eat a good breakfast on the morning of the test. Obviously, these students know their teachers place a great deal of importance on test achievement. Fortunate are the young writers who know their teacher places a priority on writing—not writing to achieve on a test, but writing to communicate with an audience. These students enjoy writing and want to write, the first steps toward writing fluency.

Non-writers frequently see fluency as the last stage in a three-step process:

Step 1:   The writer works to achieve correctness, focusing on the mechanics of grammar, spelling, and punctuation, as a foundation for good writing.

Step 2:   Next, the writer works on such writing issues as clarity, organization, word choice, effective lead elements, and voice.

Step 3:   Finally, the writer continues to write using the skills and competencies developed in the first two steps until he or she has achieved fluency.

Those are the same three steps many teachers are using in their writing workshops. But most writers will tell you that this paradigm is standing on its head. Writing works in exactly the *opposite* way:

Step 1:   First, we develop fluency by letting writers write in authentic settings that emphasize writing used to communicate with an audience—to tell a story or to pass along information. Writing is a daily activity across the curriculum. Students see themselves as writers because they write and many of their pieces are published.

Step 2:   In the context of writing, we work on writing competencies. Students who know they are writing for an audience will be interested in making that writing as good as possible. They will want to see how other writers handle leads for their narratives. They want to look at how their favorite authors use dialogue and set a scene through effective description. They delight in learning new words in their reading and seeing how authors use words to paint pictures.

Step 3: Because they are involved in the editing of their work, they want to know more about grammar and spelling and punctuation. They come to share a writer's view of mechanics—that they are aids to readability.

Fluency is perhaps the most important quality a young writer can bring to a writing achievement test. Fluent writers are accustomed to the writing process. They tend to work faster because they have more practice. They have more writing models in their head. And they are more confident of their abilities because they have enjoyed the validation of seeing their books published.

Reference

Atwell, N. (1998). *In the middle*. 2nd edition. Portsmouth, NH: Heinemann.

Workshop 3

What *is* good writing anyway?
Using Children's Literature to Teach Writing

❖ ❖ ❖ ❖ ❖ ❖ ❖

Nothing frustrates a young writer—or an older writer—more than looking at a finished piece and knowing it isn't very good, but not knowing what to do about it.

It's easy to suggest that a passage sounds awkward, or that characters don't come alive, or that a plot is hard to follow. Identifying problems has never been a difficulty for writing teachers. The difficulty lies in how to fix them.

And this is never more relevant than for students who will soon be taking a writing achievement test. If writing samples are mechanically clean and follow a basic organizational pattern and carry out the instructions of the prompt, student writers typically score a passing grade. Schools where the emphasis has been on that passing grade sometimes adopt a formula approach, like Power Writing,[1] and see almost immediate results as students apply the formula to the test.

The next year, these schools expect continued improvement, but it frequently doesn't come. The formula was sufficient for an immediate boost in scores, but formula writing reads like what it is: the literary equivalent of a paint-by-numbers set.

Students also can't help but notice that the literature they enjoy wasn't put together with a "First . . . next . . . last" formula. The alternative to specific writing formulas and vague directions to "improve this paragraph" or "reword that sentence to make it better" is found in every classroom. It's the literature children love. It's John Reynolds Gardiner's *Stone Fox* and Lois Lowry's *The Giver* and Gary Paulsen's *Hatchet* and countless examples from our own adult read-

ing—books and magazines and poems and songs and even advertisements.

We have already seen the reason we read to children and let
them read on their own—to marinate them in beautiful language,
knowing that some of the vocabulary they hear, the meter and ca-
dence of the language, even the topics and perspectives of the writers, will become a part of their own thinking. One writer (Whitehead,
1968) told how children unconsciously assimilate aspects of what
they hear and read:

> Teachers who read to boys and girls . . . will, in the
> process, expose them to the full beauty and flavor of
> the English language. Indeed, children often recog-
> nize immediately a melodious, rhythmic, or emotional
> word or phrase . . . and thousands of . . . such lan-
> guage elements have been memorized instantly by
> children. (p. 81).

But good writing teachers don't let it stop there. They actively
use literature as a writing model, and help children identify the
characteristics of good writing found in the books they enjoy.

Rick Kilcup shows how he uses this principle with his 5th graders in Bellevue, Washington:

"I had read a research article about how students who discussed how authors developed characters in their favorite books
could then use these 'insider tricks' in their writing. It sounded good,
so I decided to give it a try.

"Over the next several weeks I read the class a couple of novels
written by Bill Wallace. We talked about his ability to leave you
hanging at the end of the chapter, making you want more. We talked
about his masterful use of comparison. The class was quick to pick
up on such passages as 'It (a panther) raced through the glistening
powder . . . like a shadow on the snow' brought his stories to life.

"I wondered if the research was correct and if our discussions
would spill over into my students' writing. I got my answer that spring.
Each year, our fifth graders take a district-wide writing test. They
are given a topic and two and one-half hours spread over two days.
All brainstorming, drafting, revising, and editing are to be done without help. About halfway through the ordeal, I was wandering around
the room feeling useless when one of my boys headed my way tot-
ing his story and wearing a sly grin. When I reminded him that I
was off-limits, he told me that he didn't need help but just wanted to
read me part of his story.

"The sentence he shared contained a beautiful comparison. As
he walked away, I wondered if his effective use of that comparison

> were in any way related to our discussions of Bill Wallace novels. I knew it was when he stopped, turned back toward me, and whispered, 'Eat your heart out, Bill Wallace.'"

What Rick Kilcup did with his fifth graders was to take the novels they already enjoyed and examine the reason for their impact. In other words, why was the writing effective? Good writing teachers do not analyze every story their read to their classes—dissecting every story would take the enjoyment out of experiencing a new book and send the message that books are written to be analyzed, not appreciated.

But neither do we want to miss the teachable moments that come from taking a story children love and showing them what the writer did to make it such a great read. That will lead to discussions of word choice, organization, figurative language, lead construction, effective dialogue, and other points of style.

Teachers whose classes face writing achievement tests find that using real literature as a writing model is a great alternative—and a more effective instructional strategy—than having students write to canned formats and complete writing worksheets.

Approaches vary, but a typical lesson strategy might look like this:

Step 1:   Share the book, or use an effective selection from a basal that all students are reading. You might have other activities related to the book that help students see why it is so effective. For instance, Bill Martin Jr.'s *Ghost-Eye Tree* is a great example of effective use of dialogue, and as such it lends itself to being acted out. Let a group act out the book, with each character speaking the words of his or her character in quotations. The boy who narrates *Ghost-Eye* also speaks to himself about his feelings on encountering what he considers the haunted tree. The student who plays the boy in the classroom drama might also read the boy's thoughts, or a narrator might take that part. But later, you will want to explain that the author inserted the boy's thoughts to show the reader what was going through his mind, in addition to what he said. And you'll want to share that, when a writer does that, it's called *interior monologue.* You might have them go back to a piece they have already written that contains dialogue and insert some interior monologue. And if you just want to illustrate dialogue, *Ghost-Eye* is an effective example of telling a story through the interactions of two characters.

Step 2: After you read the story, conduct a discussion that focuses on the lesson you plan to teach based on the book. For instance, if you want to discuss descriptive writing, you might read from Ray Bradbury's *Dandelion Wine* (1957):

> It was a quiet morning, the town covered over with darkness and at ease in bed. Summer gathered in the weather, the wind had the proper touch, the breathing of the world was long and warm and slow. You had only to rise, lean from your window, and know that this was indeed the first real time of freedom and living, this was the first morning of summer.
>
> Douglas Spaulding, 12, freshly wakened, let the summer idle him on its early-morning stream. Lying in this third-story cupola bedroom, he felt the tall power it gave him, riding high in the June wind, the grandest tower in town. At night, when the trees washed together, he flashed his gaze like a beacon from this lighthouse in all directions over swarming seas of elm and oak and maple. (p. 11)

Don't ask a general question, like "Did you like the story?" Instead, if you're focusing on descriptive writing, you might ask what they thought about when they heard the selection. Have them close their eyes and read a section again. Ask what they saw in their minds. Then ask how Ray Bradbury painted that picture with words. Type a few paragraphs and let students find the words and phrases the writer used to make the setting and character come alive. You might also try rewriting the section in more mundane language—language that tells but doesn't show. Here's how you might do it with the Bradbury piece:

> Douglas Spaulding woke up on the first day of summer. Doug loved the first day of summer because he was free to do what he wanted to. The town was quiet when Douglas woke up, like a typical early summer day.

Compare your rewritten version with the original. Let your young writers show you what the author did to make the images play in your mind, to remind you of similar summer days you have experienced.

Step 3: Now you're ready to write. If the lesson was on dialogue, you might let them imagine an argument between themselves and someone else. Let them identify on paper who they argued with and what the argument was about. Then you might ask, "When you had the argument, who spoke first, and what was the very first thing said that started it all? Write that down." What your young writers have at this point is the first sentence in a dialogue. Now let them write. You may come back tomorrow with another lesson on punctuating dialogue, followed by an opportunity to edit what they have written. They can keep their argument-dialogue in their writing folders and come back later and insert interior monologue when you talk about that in a writer's craft mini-lesson. Or they can write a lead for a story that includes the argument when you talk about lead writing.

Obviously, this is not a complete writing program. Young writers should have many opportunities to choose their own topics. But if you use craft lessons based on literature, children will use those ideas when they write their own original pieces. In one-on-one conferences, you can refer back to those craft lessons you did earlier.[2] And if you make notes on chart paper during the lesson, you can tell a child who is having trouble with description to go to your chart file and pull the one on descriptive writing for help and ideas.

The key in using craft lessons from literature is to illustrate how authors use those techniques to make meaning, not just to present them as illustrations of skills children need to learn. Lucy Calkins (1994) has noted that losing sight of our ultimate objective in teaching these skills can turn even our references to great writing into contrived exercises: "To study alliteration or parallelism as ends in themselves is to misunderstand these techniques, for their power comes from using them to create meaning" (p. 353).

But illustrating techniques and principles of good writing from children's literature helps young writers to see how authors use those techniques to bring books to life. If young writers are not writing every day themselves, they will find these lessons interesting but irrelevant. But if they are writing every day, they will inevitably use what they have learned.

Notes

[1]   See pp. 70–71 for a discussion of Power Writing and other formula approaches to writing.

[2] You can find a number of books that share mini-lesson ideas on writing techniques illustrated in children's literature. Some examples include: J. Clemmons, and L. Laase, *Language arts mini-lessons: Step-by-step skill-builders for your classroom.* New York: Scholastic, 1995; J. Stewig, *Read to write: Using children's literature as a springboard for teaching writing.* New York: Richard C. Owen, 1980; R. Culham, *Picture books: An annotated bibliography with activities for teaching writing.* Portland, OR: Northwest Regional Educational Laboratory, 1998; R. Fletcher, and J. Portalupi, *Craft lessons.* Portsmouth, NH: Heinemann, 1998.

References

Bradbury, R. (1957). *Dandelion wine.* New York: Doubleday & Company, Inc.

Calkins, L. (1994). *The art of teaching writing.* Portsmouth, NH: Heinemann.

Whitehead, R. (1968). *Children's literature: Strategies of teaching.* Englewood Cliffs, NJ: Prentice-Hall.

WORKSHOP 4

Using Test Rubrics to Teach Writing

When Mrs. Ramirez asks her third graders what they will be writing about in Monday's writing workshop, Spencer's hand is the first to go up. She smiles at this response from one of her most reluctant writers, curious as to what motivated Spencer's desire to write.

"We won our soccer game Saturday," he begins, without waiting to be called on.

"I made three assists. I'm going to write about it."

Mrs. Ramirez watched out of the corner of her eye as Spencer wrote. It didn't take him long to finish his piece and put down his pencil. He knew that in Mrs. Ramirez' class, when you finished a piece in writer's workshop you either re-read your piece to see how you could improve it or began work on another piece.

Spencer couldn't see any way his soccer story could be improved, so he looked in his writing folder at a topics list he had been compiling to see what else he could do until writing time was up and he could share his piece with the class.

When share time began, his hand was again the first to go up. He read his piece to his fellow third grader writers:

> Saterday I had a soccer game. In the first half we where losey 2 to 1 but in the second half we tied it up and then won the game 3 to 2. We played town and conutry. I made three asits. One of are goles was off sides but if it wanstn't we would of won 2 to 4. I played stricker and center mid. Bobby, scott, matt, and mike scored a gole Scott scored on a cornner kick and other threee where just by pasing. My number was 13. The other team parents where saying whatch

out for number 13 in spanish. My mom hered them and they where saying where going to beat this team 5 to 1. We where playing on the Hollohan field grass. My team mates are matt, scott, mike, Bobby, Spencer, Deven, Ryan, Kelly, natherroy, greg, Andrew and Drew.

A piece like Spencer's gives writing teachers an opportunity to accomplish two objectives: (1) to show students what good writing is and how they can apply those characteristics of good writing to their pieces, and (2) to help them prepare for state writing achievement tests.

Actually, those two goals are really the same—the best preparation for state writing achievement tests is understanding what effective writing really is.

The state tests generally define good writing in a rubric.

What's a rubric?

A rubric is a system used to determine how well a task has been performed.

The system consists of a set of criteria by which the task will be assessed, a strategy for applying those criteria, and labels or score points that allow the task to be assessed on a continuum.

For example, the Florida Writing Assessment Program rubric uses the elements of effective writing (focus, organization, support, and conventions) as the criteria and a holistic strategy for determining the overall quality of the writing on a continuum of 1 through 6.

Other rubrics may use labels, such as "exemplary," "high," "medium," and "low," rather than numerical values to communicate the relative success of the task.

For an example of a rubric written so that young writers can use it to improve their writing, see Colorado's "Kid-Friendly Rubric" on pages 32–34.

Students in Mrs. Ramirez' Florida classroom do not know about the Florida Writes rubric, designed to guide evaluation of the statewide test. But they do know about the prominently displayed chart in their room, "Characteristics of Good Writing" (see Figure 3.1). When they read trade books, they find elements of those books that fit those characteristics. When Mrs. Ramirez asks students why they like a book, they frequently refer to the chart ("I like the way the book keeps you interested all the way through by just sticking to the story and not putting a bunch of extra stuff in").

But Mrs. Ramirez' "Characteristics of Good Writing" chart contains all the elements of the Florida Writes rubric—so every opportunity to look at improving a piece of writing is really also an exercise in preparing for the test.

How to think like a writer

The characteristics
of good writing

√   It has purpose, focus, a clear theme.

√   Its organization makes sense; it follows a clear order
    and logical sequence.

√   It is written so that the reader can picture the action
    and the setting and actually hear the characters speak-
    ing; it *shows* rather than tells; strong verbs bring the
    piece to life.

√   It's written for readablity; it has varied and accurate
    word choice; sentence length and type is varied; it
    makes effective use of literary devices.

√   It uses reader-friendly conventions—grammar, spell-
    ing, punctuation, usage.

Figure 3.1

After Spencer shared his piece, there were lots of questions.

"What happened when Scott got a corner kick?" Eli asked, prompting Spencer to talk excitedly about the action near the goal. Soon, he was retelling the story of the game, describing in vivid detail the action leading up to the goals and announcing each with a resounding "GOAL!" His classmates listened attentively.

Spencer grinned. He was clearly pleased that his friends were so interested in his story about the soccer game. Mrs. Ramirez also smiled, realizing that Spencer was hooked on telling his story, and now she could talk with him about revising it.

"Spencer, you have just told such an exciting story about your soccer game," she said. "You described the action so well that I felt like I was there to see those goals and cheer for your team. Have you thought about writing what you just told us into your story? It would make it even more exciting!

"Let's look at how you could organize your piece so your readers could follow the game action even better," she added. Placing a simple graphic organizer on the overhead projector, she continued to support Spencer by making notes about the soccer game action on the transparency as he talked. Her comments reflected the language of the "characteristics of good writing chart" as she guided the discussion, gently helping him to weave his supporting details into the organizational plan.

Spencer was now ready to revise his story, a revision more likely to produce an effective piece of writing that will connect with his readers and give Spencer great practice in writing the type of narrative that scores well on the state test. Spencer's writing improves each time Mrs. Ramirez uses this technique with the class.

But Mrs. Ramirez knows that Spencer and several others in the class are making the same kinds of errors with conventions. She pulls them together in a small group for a mini-lesson and some work with the "w" words that they find so challenging. At the end of this small group session, they add the words to their personal dictionaries for future use.

Across the hallway, in Mr. Wilson's fourth grade class, the students are preparing for the upcoming state writing achievement test. Ashley, who was in Mrs. Ramirez' class last year, is an accomplished and confident writer. In her response to an expository prompt, she has written:

> All of us have to follow lunchroom rules or it would not be a perfect lunchroom because all the kids would think they could do whatever they wanted to do. If kids followed lunchroom rules it would prevent chaos, yelling, and trash.
>
> You need lunchroom rules or there would be chaos everywhere. For instance, everyone would be running around like the Olimpix Athleites with a soccer ball under there toes. Kids carring their lunch trays would spill it all over them. If you spilt your food all over, you wouldn't eat it because it's on your outside instead of your inside.
>
> If you yelled in the lunchroom, do you know how many kids that would be yelling? At my school that's about 240 kids yelling! You couldn't even hear yourself think and you might loose your hearing.
>
> If we didn't have lunchroom rules trash would be all over the floor. For example, when it was time to leave to go back to your classroom and you didn't throw your trash away another kid might swipe off the table. You would have to trample through it. You would not be able to walk without getting mustard on your brand new shoes. Once I got school pizza on the bottom of my shoes. It gave me the creeps.
>
> Well, I hope you have learned why schools need lunchroom rules. So there would not be chaos, yelling and trash. You can make your school better with lunchroom rules!

Ashley enjoys sharing her writing and gives Mr. Wilson permission to share it with the class on the overhead projector. After reading the essay orally, Ashley and the teacher invite the class to comment on her essay. A lively discussion follows, with several students offering their own stories about spills and disgusting messes.

The students are accustomed to responding to writing in terms of the characteristics of good writing and Emily begins:

"Ashley, everything in your paper was about the lunchroom rules. There wasn't any other stuff in there."

"It was more fun to read about what happens without rules than the boring stuff if everybody followed rules. That was a good way to organize," Ryan said.

"Maybe you could tell some more details about the food being on the outside than the inside and that would make it more interesting. You could even make it funny," suggested Jeremy, who always looks for ways to make the class laugh.

Ashley responded: "That's the hardest part for me. I just don't know what to say about it."

Mr. Wilson listens to his students as they talk to Ashley as one writer to another. He feels reassured. While her paper is not perfect, he knows that she and her classmates are well prepared for the state test because they understand what good writing is and they write every day.

Mrs. Ramirez and Mr. Wilson have succeeded in teaching their students to use the characteristics of good writing in their work. They have also helped their writers to make the connection between those characteristics and the rubric by which their writing will be evaluated. Weaving revision strategies into the discussions of the papers also helps reduce test anxiety by giving young writers tools to use in their writing. And by the time Mr. Wilson's students take their writing test, the rubric that will be used to assess their work has already become a part of their thinking.

The Kid-Friendly 4-Point Rubric for Students

4 points: My writing is clear and does what the prompt asked me. My errors in spelling and punctuation are so few they wouldn't bother you.

Content and Organization

- I used important details and information.
- I did not forget or lose the main idea when I added interesting details.
- I was careful to organize the ideas logically and effectively.
- I made sure all of my details connect to the prompt.

Style

- My word choice is awesome. The words fit the prompt well.
- I tried to use interesting words or descriptions to make pictures in the reader's mind.
- My sentences are not all the same. I used different sentences.
- My writing is neat and almost perfect.

3 points: My writing is pretty good. I did what the prompt asked of me, but I did not give enough information or details with my answer. I need to add more. I made very few errors in spelling and punctuation.

Content and Organization

- I explained my main idea, but I need to add more information. I need to choose more important details and take out those that aren't.
- Sometimes my writing moves away from the main point or details get in the way of the main point.
- I need to put my story in order.
- I need to connect ideas so that they all fit well together.

Style

- Most of my words go well with the purpose.
- At times I could have chosen better words.
- My sentences are well written, but I did not try different kinds of sentences.
- Most of my paper is neat and easy to read.
- I may have made a mistake in grammar, spelling, or punctuation, but you can still understand what I mean.

2 points: My writing is not clear enough, and I drifted away from the prompt. I need to use more details and be sure they are accurate. I did not notice the errors I made in spelling and mechanics.

Content and Mechanics

- I need to write more clearly and be sure I keep the purpose in mind. I need to be sure I have told all that I can to make my paper complete.
- I may have not included enough details, or I may have spent too much time on the details and forgot the purpose.
- My writing may seem more like a list than like a paragraph with ideas that go together.
- I need to make sure my writing stays on topic.

Style

- I need to use words that are strong and effective.
- My writing is not smooth, and I repeat myself at times.
- Sometimes you can't read my writing, and I need to be more careful about spelling and mechanics.

1 point: My writing needs to be focused and organized. I need to write more to the prompt and include a lot more details and information. I have too many mistakes in spelling and mechanics.

Content and Organization

- I have not paid enough attention to what I am supposed to write.
- I need to include a lot more information.
- I need to organize my ideas so that my writing is clear.
- I need to make sure my writing is complete and about the topic.

Style

- I need to write so that others can read it.
- I need to choose a variety of words and be sure that they are just right.
- I need to learn more words.
- I need to write complete sentences.
- My mistakes in spelling and mechanics keep my reader from understanding what I meant.

Used by permission of the Colorado State Department of Education

WORKSHOP 5

Teaching Narrative and Expository Writing

Most state writing assessments require that students follow the directions of a prompt to write either a narrative or expository draft. Narratives tell a personal or fictional story; exposition explains a concept, defines, instructs, or persuades.

Test-writers typically construct prompts that orient students to the writing situation being presented and then give them directions for their writing assignment. A handbook for Florida teachers on the state's writing assessment (*Florida Writes! Report on the 1998 Assessment,* 1998) gives examples of typical narrative and expository prompts: (p. 3)

> [Narrative:] Everyone has done something that he or she will always remember.
>
> Before you begin writing, think about a time you did something that you will always remember.
>
> Now tell the story about the time you did something that you will always remember.
>
> [Expository:] Everyone has jobs or chores.
>
> Before you begin writing, think about one of your jobs or chores.
>
> Now explain why you do your job or chore.

Students have a limited amount of time to consider the prompt, organize their thoughts, come up with a writing plan, draft their piece, and perhaps leave a little time at the end for revision and editing. Obviously, it is important that students be comfortable with both narrative and expository formats.

Teaching Narrative Writing

Children began learning how to write narratives when they heard their first stories as a baby. Imitation plays a key part in learning any form of writing, and that is especially true with narrative writing because children have heard so many narratives by the time teachers first introduce and teach narratives as a writing form.

Three steps are important in learning to write narratives:

Step 1: The groundwork for understanding, for developing a "sense of story," is laid by hearing and reading the work of many storytellers. This gives young writers a *schema*, a frame of reference, for understanding how stories work. Hearing and reading stories must continue throughout the writer's development. At first, the narratives one has heard form an unconscious backdrop for the instruction that is being given—they provide a mental frame of reference for words like *plot* and *character* and *setting*. But then, as writers begin to learn how narratives are crafted and then write narratives themselves, the stories they read and hear take on new meaning. Indeed, they come to enjoy stories in a way that only writers can; that is, they appreciate the way the author *crafted* the story, used dialogue to move the plot along, or created a unique plot twist. In other words, they come to read like writers.

Step 2: We begin now to teach the various elements of narrative:

- **Plot:** What happened?

- **Setting:** Where did it happen? How is it described? How important is setting for this story?

- **Characterization:** What are the characters like? How can you tell? How does the author show what the characters are like?

- **Theme:** What is the story really about? Fables may state the theme explicitly; in other stories it may be stated implicitly. Stories like *Goldilocks and the Three Bears* and *The Three Little Pigs* lend themselves to discussion of what the author was really trying to say by telling this story.

- **Point of View:** This is the stance the author takes in the story. Is the author *omniscient,* seeing and knowing everything, but not a part of the story itself? Or is the story told from first person (I), second person (you), or third person (she, he, they)? Books like John Scieszka's *The True Story of the Three Little Pigs* (1989)*,* which takes a story traditionally told by a third-person storyteller and tells it from the wolf's point of view, can show the impact of point-of-view shifts in narrative.

Step 3: We also teach how stories are crafted. Even though young writers have developed story-sense by hearing and reading many stories and watching many stories on movies and TV, they still need help in learning how to tell stories themselves. Several strategies can give young writers the tools they need to put their stories on paper:

- *Most stories have a problem or conflict.* It may be a conflict between characters, between characters and a group of people, between characters and nature, or within the character. Review the class's favorite stories and identify the conflict. Then look to see when the conflict is introduced by the author. Typically, that will take place early in the story, not after a long detailing of the setting or descriptions of characters that don't relate to the problem at hand. For instance, you might want to read the first two paragraphs of Beverly Cleary's *Ribsy* (1964), a fourth-grade favorite: (pp. 7–8)

> Henry Huggins' dog Ribsy was a plain ordinary city dog, the kind of dog that strangers usually called Mutt or Pooch. They always called him this in a friendly way, because Ribsy was a friendly dog. He followed Henry and his friends to school. He kept the mailman company. He wagged his tail at the milkman, who always stopped to pet him. People liked Ribsy, and Ribsy liked people. Ribsy was what you might call a well-adjusted dog.
>
> This did not mean that Ribsy had no troubles. He did have troubles, and high on the list were fleas, particularly one mean hungry flea that persistently nipped Ribsy right under his collar where he could not get at it no matter how hard he scratched with his hind foot. If it had not been for that flea, things might have been different for Ribsy.

> Ribsy's troubles began one Saturday morning in October. . . .

Show your students that the conflict that led to Ribsy's troubles was introduced in the second paragraph of the story. Cleary does not spend a lot of time describing Ribsy and Henry. Instead, she immediately introduces a problem, and that's what keeps the reader interested.

Try taking characters at random that students make up—like a fourth grade girl at school, a kindergarten child in a supermarket, a bear in the forest. First describe those characters. Tell what they look like, how they are dressed, what they are like (brave, timid, happy-go-lucky, etc.). Then, give the character a problem. When you have a character and a problem, you have the makings of a story.

- *The plot is made up of basic story parts—setting, conflict, and resolution.* Story maps that picture the sequence of events in a story can help young writers see how they fit together:

  — Stories frequently begin with an introduction of characters and setting. This part of a story can be fairly short, just long enough to set up the reader for the conflict to follow. Review the first paragraph of *Ribsy* above and note that Cleary introduces both Ribsy and Henry. She doesn't describe how either looks or give much information about them. Instead, she gives us the information we need to relate to the problem to come—"character" information about Ribsy. After the first paragraph we know that Ribsy is a friendly dog, that people like him, and that he's a "well-adjusted dog." Once we know that, she is ready to introduce the problem of this otherwise-contented canine: fleas, and one in particular.

  — Next comes the problem or conflict. This can take place at one time and place or over a span of time in a variety of places. In *The Three Little Pigs*, the conflict was the wolf's assault on the pigs' houses to capture them and eat them. The conflict actually occurred at each pig's house as the wolf huffed and puffed and eventually blew the first two houses down. As characters attempt to solve a problem or escape a conflict, they will typically encounter roadblocks or temporary setbacks, which may actually make the problem worse. The conflict builds to a high point, where the problem is about to be solved.

- *The story ends with a conclusion or solution.* The problem is solved and the roadblocks overcome to end the story.

When students develop a vocabulary that includes these story elements—and when they see how these elements have been used by authors in the books and stories they are already familiar with—it is easier to adopt them in their own prose.

Not all narratives will have a problem or conflict.[1] Note, for example, the Florida standardized test writing prompt at the beginning of this chapter. It asks writers to tell about a memorable event in their lives. That event may involve conflict, like the time the student performed in a ballet recital to the cheers of the audience or got a hit to win a ballgame. One involves a conflict with fear or nervousness, and the other a conflict with a pitcher trying to strike the batter out. But what if a student's memory involves a fun day at grandpa's farm, a day spent fishing and exploring and learning to milk a cow? No conflict there.

So expose children to narratives that do not involve conflict, like Byrd Baylor's *I'm in Charge of Celebrations* (1986), about the author's days in the desert and how she has come to celebrate desert life, and Gloria Houston's *My Great-Aunt Arizona* (1992), which recounts the life and contributions of a schoolteacher in the Appalachian Mountains. For narratives like these, make a time line of the major events. Pay special attention to how the author begins the story—what lead he or she uses to lure the reader into this story—and to the conclusion of the story.

A student responding to the prompt about the memorable day, for instance, might immediately think of the day on grandpa's farm. The student will then realize that this won't be a story containing a problem, but a narrative of significant events. She might use clustering or webbing to quickly organize her thinking. In her cluster, she quickly lists what she did at grandpa's farm: got up before sunrise, rode a tractor, milked a cow, went exploring and found a bees' nest, played with a girl from a neighboring farm, and went fishing and caught two catfish. The author realizes that this is too much to put in a narrative, that she needs to select only the best parts. She chooses milking the cow, finding the bees' nest, and catching the fish. Already thinking like a writer, she knows that these will also have a lot of visual images that make them easy to describe. The author now has the three main events of her narrative, which she will write about chronologically, as they occurred. Now all that she needs is a beginning to draw the reader into her story and an ending to wrap it up.

Intermediate writers just beginning to write narratives often find them difficult. Don Graves (1989) notes that children learn to write narratives just like they learn to draw; that is, they begin with a caricature of the narrative (p. 51). Boys, especially, write narratives with good guys and bad guys and lots of action that ends quickly. This is a necessary developmental stage for young writers. As teachers, we continue to model narrative writing, to illustrate with well-told narratives in trade books, and to demonstrate in craft lessons how writers use dialogue, setting, conflict, and so on to tell stories.

Effective writing teachers realize that when it comes to narrative writing, you learn what stories are by listening to them, by reading them, by telling them, and by writing them. And once you begin to write stories, each new story you hear or read or tell helps to extend your understanding and broaden your definition of the craft of narrative writing.

Teaching Expository Writing

Children's first encounters with print are typically with narratives. In school, however, they discover that authors do more than just tell stories—they also pass along a fascinating world of information designed to explain, persuade, and provide information and directions. Intermediates' encounters with expository text range from instruction manuals for their computer games to fascinating illustrated explanations of the Egyptians' process of mummification to books and pamphlets produced by the DARE (Drug and Alcohol Resistance Education) organization explaining the dangers of experimenting with drugs. Teachers who think intermediates always prefer narratives over expository texts have not exposed their students to enough well-written and engagingly illustrated books on topics that are interesting to them. The teacher who brings to class David Schwartz's (1995) *Yanomami*, a book about a tribe in the Amazon jungle illustrated with color photographs of life in the village, or Stephen Biesty's (1995) *Castle*, which includes detailed diagrams of medieval castles, will soon discover that expository texts are as fascinating to children as narratives.[2]

Expository text structure is different from the organization of a narrative. Rather than telling a story, expository texts explain facts and present ideas by organizing them in terms of their logical relationship to each other.

Expository forms typically fall into one of several types:

- **Direction** tells the reader how to do something by outlining the steps involved. A computer manual or a book on how to care for your class hedgehog is an example of this form.

- **Persuasion** attempts to convince a reader to accept a certain point of view. A class-written letter to the editor of your local paper or a letter to the principal urging her to keep the computer lab open after school are examples.

- **Description** tells about a person, place, thing, action, or event, such as a book about the animals of Antarctica that names and describes the animals, their feeding habits, and their habitats.

- **Expression** focuses on the attitudes and beliefs of the writer. Bill Martin's (1998) book *The Turning of the Year* goes through the year month by month, giving an impression of each month in the lyrical prose for which this great storyteller is known so well.

Expository texts are frequently approached in terms of problems and solutions, comparisons and contrast, lists and explanations, cause and effect, and sequence. Helping students identify the approach used in texts they know can show them their options when they approach an opportunity to craft an expository text themselves. For instance, a computer manual might be organized according to problems and solutions, showing how to troubleshoot various computer glitches. A student who takes tae kwon do might have a book that contrasts karate and kung fu. A cheerleader might have a manual that explains each cheer and its actions in sequence.

Young writers can easily learn to analyze a writing opportunity—or a test prompt—to see what expository approach is needed. Take, for instance, the expository prompt presented at the beginning of this chapter, which called for a student to "explain why you do your job or chore." Obviously, the prompt is calling for a piece of descriptive exposition—to list and describe the reasons why the author performs a chore. The writer can approach this in a number of ways: perhaps a simple list of reasons with explanations, a problem/solution piece in which the writer talks about a need around the house and how he or she can best meet it, or perhaps as a cause/effect situation, listing the positive consequences that come when the chore is done right and on time and the negative consequences when it is neglected.

What steps can be taken to produce a good piece of expository writing in response to a test prompt? Students can easily implement these:

Step 1: Show students how to determine what the prompt is really looking for. Does it ask what, or why, or how? Or perhaps is it asking the writer to persuade or convince? In the prompt at the beginning of the chapter, the key words were "explain why."

Step 2: Demonstrate brainstorming, clustering, or webbing. For the "chores" prompt, the writer might first write the names of a couple of household jobs or chores. Then, at the top of the page, he or she might write "Why?" Under each chore, the writer can quickly brainstorm reasons for doing the chore—reasons that might include getting paid, pleasing mom or dad, avoiding punishment, providing a needed service around the house, earning extra privileges, and so forth.

Step 3: Then, the writer should decide which of those ideas should be included in the expository piece. That decision may be based on time available for writing, or perhaps areas the writer thinks he or she can explain best. The writer can then mark out those reasons he or she does not plan to include.

Step 4: The writer can now number the reasons in the order in which they will be used in the expository piece. The writer knows that for each reason given, he or she must elaborate, giving additional evidence—details and examples—to support the argument of the piece.

Step 5: Now it's time to write!

These steps can easily be adapted for how-to pieces, persuasive essays, or other types of expository texts.

The ideas outlined previously in this chapter for learning to write narrative also work, appropriately adapted, for learning to write expository texts. As students must develop a "sense of story" to understand how to craft a narrative, they should also develop a "sense of exposition" to feel comfortable in writing expository essays. When you read expository texts to your students, go back later and point out how the piece was organized. If you get a memo on fire drill procedures, show students that this is a meaningful example of expository writing. The goal is to help students understand what to do in case of fire. The organizational pattern used might be a chronological listing of steps to take when the fire alarm bell is sounded. Show students how the memo is organized by recounting in order the actions everyone is to perform. Look at how the memo is introduced, the lead, and how it ends, the conclusion.

As students develop a "feel" for expository texts, go on to teach them the elements of exposition. In studying narrative, they learned about plot and setting and characterization. In exposition, they will learn about description, persuasion, direction, and expression. Lead them to find these elements in expository texts.

Then, teach them how exposition is crafted. Be careful not to portray exposition only as a category of writing they need to learn in order to succeed on a test. Instead, use expository writing for meaningful projects. If first grade is studying the solar system, your class might write a book on the planets, using language and concepts first graders are likely to understand. If the finches in your class just hatched baby birds that will now be given away to good homes, the class might write a book on the care and feeding of baby finches. If your school has a newspaper, your students will enjoy writing reviews of movies, TV shows, books, CDs, and video games. Students also like to write letters to the editor of local newspapers and magazines. If a student complains that a toy or piece of software did not live up to its advertisements, you can show how a complaint letter is written. Meaning-centered writing helps students to see the real-world value of writing expository texts.

The previous pages have listed a number of strategies for teaching both narrative and expository writing. But the ideas in Workshop 1 still form the foundation for effective teaching of both writing forms: a classroom atmosphere permeated with great narrative and expository texts and full of reasons to write is the key to motivating good writing in these genres.

Notes

[1]   Some teachers differentiate narrative and story. They define story as having a plot with a problem and a solution, as opposed to a narrative, which has a plot but no problem. Another way to look at this genre might be that all stories are narratives (because they have plots), but not all narratives are stories (because they don't have problems).

[2]   Other expository texts that hook many students on this genre are Seymour Simon's books on the solar system, earthquakes, deserts, volcanos, storms, mountains, and the desert, all published by Mulberry Books. The *Eyewitness Books* series, published by Alfred A. Knopf, is another engaging and beautifully illustrated series intermediates enjoy. And to see how one author has worked expository text into narratives, see Joanna Cole's *Magic School Bus* series, published by Scholastic.

References

Baylor, B. (1995). *I'm in charge of celebrations.* New York: Aladdin.

Cleary, B. (1964). *Ribsy.* New York: Dell.

Florida writes! Report on the 1998 assessment. (1998). Tallahassee, FL: Department of Education.

Graves, D. (1989). *Experiment with fiction.* Portsmouth, NH: Heinemann.

Houston, G. (1992). *My great-aunt Arizona.* New York: HarperCollins.

Martin, Bill. (1998). *The turning of the year.* San Diego: Harcourt Brace.

Schwartz, David. (1995). *Yanomami.* New York: Lothrop, Lee & Shepard.

Scieszka, J. (1989). *The true story of the three little pigs.* New York: Viking Krestel.

WORKSHOP 6

More Than Just Elaboration:
Creating Experiences for Readers

❖ ❖ ❖ ❖ ❖ ❖ ❖

Inexperienced writers *tell* you a story or explain a concept. Good writers *show* you a story—reading their narratives is like watching a movie in your mind. Teachers want to encourage young writers to develop the ability to create an experience for the reader through writing that helps the reader picture setting, characters, and action. In classrooms, that is often called *elaboration*.

But elaboration means to develop in great detail or to ornament. And frequently that is exactly what students do: They add more details to fulfill the teacher's mandate to elaborate. The result? Sentences like this: *The ebony canine sauntered through the portal and into the waiting embrace of her master.* Obviously, the sentence has been put together with the help of a thesaurus by a writer who thought ebony was better than black, canine better than mutt, and portal better than door.

Young writers are sometimes encouraged to make lists of "exciting" words and "dull" words, as if words themselves were inherently exciting or dull. Short or common words are almost never found on the "exciting" list. Students in these classes are taught that statements should be whimpered or murmured or stammered or screeched, not just said. Students are told to search dialogue they have written to find synonyms for speech tags or attributions like *said*, and to substitute more colorful words.

After all, isn't that elaboration?

Not at all. The most frequent speech tag in all of literature is the simple, four-letter *said*. Nobody reads a novel and excitedly tells a friend, "You just have to read this new mystery! I've never seen such exciting speech tags!" Professional writers know that the key to involving readers is the dialogue itself, not the speech tags.

Other classrooms honor arcane words freshly found in the thesaurus, resulting in tortured writing like this:

> At the inception of the primary fabrication time-phase, the penultimate intelligence unit synthesized the hyperterrean coordinates and the concomitant geophysical locus.

Didn't the book of Genesis say it simpler, yet more elegantly?

> In the beginning, God created the heavens and the earth. (Genesis 1:1)

To help our students understand the real idea behind *elaboration*, we show them that writers seek to create experiences for their readers. We want readers to be able to step into our narratives and see what the main characters see. To do that, we must rely on the five senses, especially the sense of sight. A reader who can't visualize the scene won't experience what is happening on the page.

Writers have traditionally referred to this idea in terms of an old writer's maxim: *Show, don't tell.* That means writers must help the reader experience the narrative or picture the elements of the expository piece.

That does not mean the writer goes to a thesaurus to find longer or less-common words to fulfill a vague admonition to elaborate. It means, instead, that the writer goes to his or her experience to hear the dialogue and picture the characters or setting.

David, a Texas fourth grader, wanted to share his piece about his first time on a new amusement park roller coaster with his teacher, Ryan Mason, during writing conference time. David's piece included these sentences:

> My brother and I were sitting in the front car. I was really afraid when we started going up this big hill, but before long I was enjoying it so much that I even put my hands up in the air and didn't even hold on to the handlebar.

"David, I used to love roller coasters myself," Mr. Mason said when the young author finished reading. "Now they just make me nauseated. But when you were reading, I couldn't help but think of all the times I have been on a roller coaster."

"Really? Were you scared?"

"You bet. But that's half the fun, isn't it? Go back to the part about that first hill you went up, when you knew the coaster was going to get to the top and plunge straight down. Do you remember how you were feeling? What you were thinking?"

"I was pretty scared."

"Think back. What made you scared?"

"Well, I could see the hill just up ahead. We started going slower and slower, and I could hear the screams of the people in the car up ahead as it speeded up and went almost straight down, like falling off a cliff or something."

"Did you say anything to your brother?"

"Nope. I was too scared."

"Do you remember what you were thinking?"

"I was thinking that maybe I made a mistake by ever getting on this thing in the first place. I was wishing I could get off, but it was too late."

"David, when you just described how you were feeling and what you were thinking and the noises you heard, that put me right there in the coaster with you. It's what we talked about in the craft lesson last week about showing, not just telling. Would you like to add a paragraph or so to your piece, so that any reader could actually feel what you were feeling as you were starting that roller coaster ride?"

What Ryan Mason did, without ever using the word elaboration, was to encourage his young author to elaborate. Not by substituting words in his narrative, but by going back to his original piece and imagining what he did, what he saw, what he felt, and what he said. Notice that after he helped David to verbalize those memories in conference, he related them to a craft lesson on visual writing. Later that week, David read his piece on the roller coaster ride to his classmates. It included this paragraph:

> My brother and I were sitting in the front car. As we started up the steep hill at the beginning of the ride, I started to wonder if I had made a mistake by getting on the roller coaster. I watched the cars in front of us as they got to the top of the hill, and their train just speeded up. I heard them screaming as their car zoomed down the hill. I thought, "I might die on this thing," but it was too late to turn back by that time.

In David's revision, he stopped just summarizing the action for readers and let them experience it for themselves by writing about what he observed and what he thought. Several strategies are useful in getting young writers to add the kinds of detail that make writing come alive:

- **_Students need to see great descriptive writing in the books they enjoy._** Take passages from familiar books and demonstrate how authors made the scene come alive. Techniques to look for include writing rich with sensory detail, powerful verbs, specific nouns, realistic dialogue, vivid descriptions of characters and setting, and use of interior monologue to tell readers what the characters are thinking, as well as saying. You might take, for instance, this passage from Robert Newton Peck's (1972) *A Day No Pigs Would Die*. In this novel about a boyhood on a Vermont farm, young Robert talks about the last day of school:

> June come. I sure was happy as today was the last day of school.
>
> It was hot that afternoon. But I came racing home with my final report card all folded up in my pocket. The weather was dry as dust, and I was glad to be walking across pasture on the soft green meadowland, instead of kicking rocks the long way round by the dirt road.
>
> Way off to my right side, a wagon was coming down the long hill, headed for town. I didn't know the team or the driver. As the wagon moved along the dirt road, it blowed up clouds of dust that seemed to hang in the air behind it. Looked like the wagon was chased by a long dusty-gray snake. The driver had his coat took off, riding in his shirt with his sleeves rolled up. It looked like Isadore Crookshank who sat the seat, but I couldn't tell for sure (p. 50).

Note the techniques Peck uses to bring the passage to life for the reader:

—The little detail about having his report card "all folded up in my pocket" gives the reader a visual image of the boy.

—Note the other sensory details: "soft green meadowland," "kicking rocks," "clouds of dust that seemed to hang in the air," "looked like the wagon was chased by a long dusty-gray snake," "riding in his shirt with his sleeves rolled up."

- *Demonstrate the techniques of visual writing.* Having illustrated how writers bring their texts to life, go on to demonstrate the process that leads to that product. This would include such techniques as these:

—Vivid action verbs are the engines that give power to sentences. A sign writer at the San Diego Zoo who understood the power of verbs wrote this warning to visitors: "Please do not annoy, torment, pester, plague, molest, worry, badger, harry, harass, heckle, persecute, irk, bullyrag, vex, disquiet, grate, beset, bother, tease, nettle, tantalize, or ruffle the animals."

—Description creates a mental picture for the reader. Instead of saying they like to eat cookies, writers say they dream of Grandma's fresh homemade cookies that smell of warm sugar and cinnamon.

—Dialogue involves readers because they can hear the actual words of speakers, rather than the writer's paraphrase. Whether it's conversation or interior monologue (the thoughts of a character), readers relate to the real-life feel of quoted speech.

- ***Let your students observe as you demonstrate descriptive, sensory writing.*** Take a place they are familiar with or an incident that everyone experienced and write about it using the techniques described in this workshop. Let students make suggestions of ways to help readers picture the setting and action. Even though students might appreciate descriptive writing in trade books and understand the techniques they can use themselves, until they have observed it being done—by someone who starts with an idea and a blank page and writes until the story takes shape—they typically will not try to apply the techniques themselves.

Vivid descriptive writing is a higher-order writing skill. Despite the number of workbook exercises available that purport to teach descriptive writing by giving students an example followed by several sentences to choose a properly descriptive word, it takes time for students to begin to naturally incorporate this into their writing. But when good writing is honored in the classroom and students are given many examples of this technique as one method authors use to involve readers in good books, descriptive writing eventually begins to work its way into the students' prose. The payoffs on writing tests are significant, with an especially effective descriptive paragraph sometimes pushing a piece to a higher score point.

Reference

Peck, R. (1972). *A day no pigs would die*. New York: Dell.

WORKSHOP 7

A Potpourri of Writing Strategies:
Adding Variety to Your Writing Workshop

❖　❖　❖　❖　❖　❖　❖

Some people have green thumbs and others just can't make anything grow. But many brown thumb gardeners fail because they
don't understand basic horticulture: Plants are living things with a
variety of needs, beyond just regular watering.

The green thumb gardeners water, but they don't stop there.
They plant their seedlings at the right depth and in the right place
consistent with the plant's need for full, partial, or no sunlight. They
pull weeds. They fertilize. They prune. They spray for insects. Some
even talk to their plants. And their plants typically grow and flower.

The brown thumb neighbor looks over at the luxuriant growth
next door and then at his own wilted, growth-stunted plants and
laments out loud, "Why does he have such a great garden? After all,
I water all the time!"

Growing beautiful plants is like growing effective writers. Sometimes both gardeners and teachers look for a one-shot strategy, something to do automatically every day. Writing teachers with this
mentality look for one can't-miss strategy; it doesn't exist.

You have already read about several strategies that can re-fo-
cus your classroom into a community of writers and give your children a real advantage on your state writing test. But there's so much
more. The following strategies can add variety to your writing workshop and meet the specific needs you diagnose in your children's
writing.

Experience Writing
from Different Perspectives

Let your young authors experience different types of writing:

- *Modeled Writing.* This strategy is sometimes called "writing aloud." Teachers write on a chart or an overhead transparency to demonstrate the writing process to students. To do a modeled writing, simply let your students observe what goes on inside your head when you actually write. Verbalize every thought that comes through your mind. Begin by talking about your options for writing. List a few topics and think out loud which you'll write about. When you choose one, verbalize your reason for choosing that one over the others. Brainstorm or web or make notes about major ideas you'll want to cover. Then begin to write, letting students hear what you are thinking, even your frustrations over not getting something just right. For instance, you might write a lead sentence and then just say out loud, "I don't like that at all. But if I spend all my time making it better I still might not come up with anything I like. So I think I'll just go on and see if a better idea doesn't occur while I'm writing. Now let's see . . . what's next?" Modeled writing gives students the opportunity we frequently have when we watch craftspeople blow glass or sculpt or paint in public. We literally watch the creation come into being. But it also has the added advantage of hearing the verbalized thoughts of the writer as we watch the piece of writing being created.

- *Shared Writing.* In a shared writing, teachers and students collaborate to create a piece of writing. This time, the teacher holds the pen and students contribute ideas. The teacher's job is to "nudge" the young writers' thinking and language by raising questions and offering alternatives and stimulating their thinking.

- *Guided Writing.* In guided writing, the teacher works as a facilitator to students actually involved in writing. In contrast to shared writing, the student in a guided writing exercise actually holds the pen and does the writing. Regie Routman (1991) describes the role of the teacher in guided writing:

> Teachers [in a guided writing exercise] are supportive rather than directive, suggestive rather than prescriptive. Ownership of the writing always remains with the student. Our role is to empower writers to discover their own meanings. (p. 66)

- ***Independent Writing.*** This is the kind of writing students do on their own, working sometimes from their own self-selected topics and occasionally from prompts or assignments that the teacher gives. Modeled writing, shared writing, and guided writing help students see what writers do when they write and give them a schema for thinking about writing, a schema that becomes their mental set when they sit down to write independently.

The most effective writing classrooms are those in which teachers offer students many opportunities both to observe and to participate in the act of writing, including writing in learning logs and literature response logs, which allow children to respond to their reading and learning on paper. This builds fluency and encourages critical thinking, because students organize their thoughts and synthesize their learning to get their responses into writing.

Teach the Skills of Writing

Effective writing involves many skills—from topic selection to choosing a focus to lead writing to use of dialogue to involving the reader through the use of description to evoke visual images. When we marinate students in good literature through reading to them and examining the techniques of writers they enjoy, we have made a great start by furnishing their mental storehouses with writing models. But we then need to move on to show young writers how they can employ those writing techniques themselves.

Short instructional periods that focus on one specific writing competency, frequently called mini-lessons or craft lessons in the literature of the process writing movement, give practical help to students before they start their writing workshop for the day. Craft lessons are just that—instructions on some particular element of the writing process. When a baseball coach takes a player aside for a few minutes to demonstrate bunting and then gives the player an opportunity to lay down a bunt, the coach is providing a craft lesson. Bunting is not the most important skill in baseball, and many games go by without a player from either team bunting. But it is one skill that players need for specific game circumstances. A craft lesson on visual writing fulfills the same function. The teacher/writing coach has probably already pointed out examples of writing that evokes visual images. Perhaps the teacher has already started a chart where students have listed books or sections of books containing images that really leap off the page because of great descriptive writing. The teacher is now ready for a craft lesson showing students how they can develop that same ability to write descriptively.

Craft lessons are short, focusing on one skill. If the topic is descriptive writing, Monday's craft lesson might just take students back through several examples of great descriptive passages. On Tuesday, the lesson may focus on describing a person. On Wednesday, describing an object. On Thursday, a person, and so on.

Topics for craft lessons are as varied as the skills needed by young writers. Craft lessons may include such topics as choosing a topic, writing from another point of view, adding information for clarity, determining focus, eliminating excessive adjectives, punctuating dialogue, writing effective titles, improving transitions, and so forth.

What elements should be included in your craft lessons? Of course, this will vary with the needs and writing maturity of your class, but effective craft lessons typically include the following elements:

1. Define the skill to be covered explicitly. Give examples from literature.

2. Provide a step-by-step example of how to implement the skill, then demonstrate how to use it. For example, if the craft lesson is on lead writing, you may take a basic narrative you have written and show your young writers how they might come up with a lead that captures the reader's attention. Another effective strategy is to rewrite effective lead passages from several books the children already know and enjoy. Write it in a way an inexperienced writer might, then show how the book's author handled the lead, working with the same information. For an example of this technique, see a demonstration on page 24.

3. Give your students realistic practice in implementing the skill themselves. For lead writing, you might let them use finished pieces from their writing folders. Using the principles of lead writing you have shared and demonstrated, let them try to improve a lead from one of their earlier pieces.

4. Craft lessons are typically followed by writing workshop. During workshop that day, students will probably pay special attention to leads. But continue to refer to those principles in your conferencing in the workshops to follow.

5. Occasionally revisit earlier craft lessons. A great way to reinforce the concepts is to collect great examples, both from stories you read in class and from student work. When you do another craft lesson on lead writing, briefly review the principles you taught earlier, and then give examples of leads students have written that illustrate use of those principles.

Share Poetry Every Day

One of the best ways to improve writing test scores is to help your children discover poetry. The language and the rhythm of poetry, shared daily, eventually becomes part of the thinking of writers. Poetry is a different way of looking at the ordinary world—poets combine sound and meaning in the discipline of a poetic line and use rhyme, alliteration, imagery, and other literary devices to tell stories and share ideas.

Some teachers encourage each student to keep a poetry notebook. Each week many poems are shared in class, and students can pick their favorite and copy the poem or a portion of the poem into their notebook. Sometimes students underline words or phrases or images they like, or write a few sentences at the bottom of the page on why they chose this poem to copy into their poetry notebook.

The key to helping students enjoy poetry—and thus to appreciate it and appropriate the poets' techniques—is the enthusiastic performance of the teacher. Find poetry you like and throw yourself into performing it for your class. Poet Brod Bagert (1997) believes that teacher performance must be uninhibited:

> Perform with full expression. Become the character.
> Be a little kid and hold nothing in reserve. Remember
> that you are the model. Your performance will license
> your children to perform. (p. 9)

Helping children fall in love with poetry is helping them fall in love with the sound of language, and students who appreciate the sounds of language are typically those who go on to develop as writers. Novelist Eudora Welty said that poetry "is the school I went to in order to learn to write prose." And many teachers have discovered that children who come first to enjoy and then to write poetry become much more sensitive to the power of language and to the choices authors make when they write.

And More

Successful teachers throughout the nation are using many other strategies that boost writing test scores by building real writing competencies in their students. So pick and choose from among these proven strategies:

- Pick a story for a read-aloud you know your students will like. After a few sentences, pick a word from the text and start expanding on it with off-topic comments. Let's say you were reading from Jane Yolen's (1990) *The Devil's Arithmetic:*

> "I'm tired of remembering," Hannah said to her mother
> as she climbed into the car. She was flushed with April
> sun and her mouth felt sticky from jelly beans and
> Easter candy. (p. 3)

At that point, you might say, "I remember how much I loved jelly
beans as a child. My grandfather used to buy jelly beans and leave
them in a candy jar on his dresser. . . ." And then go on to talk a little
about your grandfather before going back to the story. Your students will either become frustrated or be unable to follow Jane Yolen's
story—probably both. At that point, you explain what happens when
writers go off-topic. Even though jelly beans were in Jane Yolen's
book and you logically flowed to your own experience with jelly beans,
it took you away from the story line. Children often do the same
thing in their writing. You can illustrate what happens by using
this strategy a few times, then writing something yourself where
you imitate the same problem as you have seen it so many times in
your students' writing. Teachers who have observed this problem
hundreds of times can easily write a piece themselves that sounds
like one of their students might have written it. This will show them
how the same problem "looks" in their narratives.

- Cut cartoons out of the newspaper and photocopy them. What
  you have is pure action and dialogue. They are a "slice of life."
  If a writer were telling the same story that the cartoon illus-
  trates, he or she would have to add a description of the setting
  and narrative to tell about the action. The speech bubbles would
  become the dialogue set into the narrative. Do a few for students so they can see how it is done. Then do a few together as
  a class activity. Then you can let students do their own—children love to tell the story of the cartoon and it really helps them
  with narrative writing.

- Bring in postcards or pictures from the front of greeting cards
  and let your young writers describe the scene. (Many clip art
  CD-ROMs produced for desktop publishing applications contain color photos perfect for this activity.) You can also pair off
  students and give one of them a postcard. He or she will describe the postcard to the other student, who cannot see the
  card. The listener will take notes so that he can eventually draw
  the scene being described. Listeners can ask questions about
  anything they want to know as they begin to draw. When they
  finish, they can compare their pictures with the original. Writers have to do what the describing child did for the listener—
  portray a scene so that others can picture it. This activity helps
  to build young writers' powers of description and helps them
  not to take basic details for granted.

References

Bagert, B. (1997). Baseball, Elvis, and rock & roll: The 5 steps of the performance method, in M. Sampson, and M. B. Sampson, *Literacy learning across the curriculum.* Commerce, TX: International Institute of Literacy Learning.

Routman, R. (1991). *Invitations: Changing as teachers and learners K-12.* Portsmouth, NH: Heinemann.

Yolen, J. (1990). *The devil's arithmetic.* New York: Puffin Books.

WORKSHOP 8

Getting Ready for the Test:
Preparing Parents, Students, and School

❖   ❖   ❖   ❖   ❖   ❖   ❖

At Brook Meadow Elementary on Florida's Gulf Coast, the faculty is committed to producing writers, not just students who can write effectively to the state's Florida Writes prompt. Look inside the classrooms and you'll find the type of writer-friendly atmosphere described in Workshop 1, along with many of the other strategies found in this book. But teachers at Brook Meadow know that high-stakes assessment brings test anxiety for many students and parents.

So the Brook Meadow faculty takes test preparation beyond producing fluent, effective writers. They implement a number of programs designed to create a positive testing climate in the homes of the students and in their classrooms.

Preparing Parents to Understand the Test

Early every year, the school holds parent forums on writing to tell parents about the state writing assessment and enlist their cooperation. The faculty wants to demystify the test for parents—just as they will for students—and to show them how they can cooperate with the school as test-time nears.

Effective parent forums demonstrate just what is expected of their children in the writing program and on the state assessment, using strategies like these:

- Explaining the school's writing program—both how teachers approach writing as a life skill and how they are preparing students for the state test;

- Explaining how the test works, the time limits and resources involved, the types of prompts that may be used;

- Explaining the rubric that will be used to evaluate the test and showing examples of effective student writing;

- Explaining some simple strategies that will help parents work with their young writers at home; and

- Encouraging parents to become actively involved in their child's writing development and to schedule conferences with their child's teacher about writing.

Some parents will never attend meetings such as these, but those who do tend to be the more active and involved parents, those whose support it is important to enlist. But what about those who do not come to meetings such as these?

- Make a videotape explaining the test. It's typically not best to video the parent meeting, unless you have an expert tape editor who can polish the finished product. Instead, get one or two teachers or administrators to film a half-hour explanation of the test, sharing the information given in the meeting. Make several copies of the tape and make it available to parents to check out from the office.

- Send home periodic newsletters or parent letters about the test, including a Frequently Asked Questions column that deals briefly with the types of questions parents ask.

- Make a program on the test available to parent-teacher organization meetings.

The key to enlisting parent help and support is communication. Remember that all advertising works on the principle of redundancy. That's why you see so many of the same print and TV ads over and over. Advertisers know that many people will not see the ad during a particular appearance. Others will see it but not be paying attention. Others will pay attention but forget. Others will remember, but misunderstand certain parts. So advertisers run many ads, and run the same ads again and again. Our impression of a product is formed from repeated exposure over a long period of time.

But schools so often have a single parent meeting and then wonder why more parents do not understand or support what they are doing. Parents do care and many will support our efforts, but we have to be persistent and offer multiple exposures to our message in many different formats.

Preparing Students to Take the Test

Fourth grade teacher Paul Wilson has heard stories of students who were paralyzed by the state test—students who "forgot all they knew" when faced with the prompt. Paul knows that the best way to help his students feel comfortable with the test is to help them feel comfortable with writing, so his class writes every day in writing workshop and across the curriculum. Paul talks to students as writers every day, and encourages, praises, and coaches their writing.

He also wants his students to understand his state's expectations for writing, so he shares writing samples that have been scored with the assessment rubric. Over the course of the year, he incorporates these samples into his craft lessons, discussing the writing in rubric language and relating it to the characteristics of good writing his children are familiar with. Paul's students soon become adept at using the rubric to evaluate their own writing.

Paul and the other members of the fourth grade team want their young writers to do well on the test, but they do not want them to come to view writing as something merely to be evaluated. They know that humans did not invent writing so American education could have something to assess in the fourth grade. Writing was invented to communicate—to tell stories and to share information. Evaluation is a part of writing, but only one part, a part that must be kept in the context of communication. Paul and his colleagues help students maintain that perspective by seeking ways to let students share their writing with others. In addition to the sharing and publication in the classrooms, they look for places in the school to display student writing. As the year progresses, writing is posted in the school office, in the hallways, and in the school cafeteria. Visitors to the principal's office find student books—not old copies of *National Geographic*—on the coffee tables in the reception area. Responses to favorite books are prominently displayed in the media center. Any space where other people, adults—as well as children— may see and read the writing becomes a place to celebrate a writer's work.

The principal even uses morning announcements to celebrate writing. Several times each week, students are selected to read a finished piece of their writing on the closed-circuit television morning show. At first, students are nervous about appearing and reading on camera. But when they see the reaction of their schoolmates, they become eager to share their writing in this manner. The faculty at a nearby school does not have closed-circuit TV equipment, but adapt the idea to their school's intercom morning announcements. Both formats provide the young writers with a larger audience for their work.

As the year progresses, Paul and his colleagues add other strategies to help students become more comfortable with the writing test experience. Florida assesses drafts, so they give more attention to showing students how to produce an acceptable piece of writing in the draft stage, instead of taking it through the entire revision and editing process. These draft-only pieces are not the staple of the writing diet in Paul's fourth grade class—most pieces are taken through the entire process. But he does offer many opportunities to do the type of on-demand, little-time-to-revise writing that students will find on the test. He relates this writing to the test students will take, but he also shows them that many types of real-world writing are quite similar to the draft written on a subject not chosen by the writer and completed under time constraints. Newspaper news stories are a good example of this type of writing, and Paul asks a local reporter to come to his class and talk about the type of writing she does. Students see that she gets assignments from an editor, has to research quickly and plan her story in her head, and then write under pressure of a deadline—much as they will have to do on their state test.

Knowing that elementary-age children do not have a well-developed sense of time, the fourth grade teachers plan for timed writing experiences to help students gain a feel for writing in the 45-minute time period prescribed for the state test. The school has purchased a "teach timer" (a timekeeping device projected on a screen by an overhead projector) to help students manage writing in the allowed time. Some fourth grade teachers, however, prefer to help students manage their time by writing time segments on the board.

Paul encourages his students to take no more than 10 minutes to plan their writing. He tells them when their first 10 minutes have elapsed, then he tells them that they have 35 minutes left to write their draft. He helps them keep track of their time, so they can have a few minutes at the end to re-read their piece and do some basic editing.

The fourth grade teachers at Paul's school also use a test facsimile to familiarize students with the format they will be expected to use. Typically, state tests will include a page to identify the student, a page for the prompt and planning, and pages for students to write on. Only writing on the designated pages is scored. The facsimile-test practice that students do in the weeks just prior to the test helps to increase their comfort level when the real test is administered.

Preparing the School to Support the Test

At Paul's school, the entire building—and even a nearby high school—share the fourth grade team's commitment to building writers and to encouraging success on the state writing assessment. The support takes a variety of forms:

- Other classes write cards and letters of encouragement to the fourth grade students, both as individual writers and as classes.

- Banners are made and posted in prominent places to let fourth graders know that the whole school is supporting them.

- The week before the test, the neighborhood high school sends its cheerleaders and a small contingent from the marching band to lead the school in a writing pep rally. The students who will be taking the test are featured in groups with music and cheers.

Then the day of the test arrives. The principal and assistant principal pull red wooden wagons loaded with milk, juice, and power breakfast bars. They enter each fourth grade class to deliver this special breakfast to get the students off to a good start on their test day, bringing words of encouragement with the food.

Each fourth grade teacher chats with the students as they enjoy their breakfast and conversation with friends. Then the school settles down to the serious business of writing. Although only the fourth grade is taking the state test, during the test time every child in every class is writing because the entire school has designated this day for writing emphasis.

In the fourth grade, the test packets are distributed. Students open them to find the familiar format they have seen several times during the last few weeks. The prompt, the limitations imposed by the test (no conferencing or outside resources like dictionaries or thesauruses), the time constraints—all echo the writing exercises students have worked on during the last several weeks. And most importantly, the students themselves are experienced, fluent writers. They have been accustomed to writing every day across the curriculum and especially in writing workshop. Though only fourth graders, they are already writing veterans.

And their writing test scores reflect the writing environment and the special preparations provided by a faculty committed both to success on the test and to authentic writing achievement in their students' lives.

WORKSHOP 9

Frequently Asked Questions:
Issues and Answers on Writing and Testing

❖ ❖ ❖ ❖ ❖ ❖ ❖

How about "teaching to the test"? Does it work? Some of my colleagues spend lots of time practicing timed writing and test prompts. Does all that test-writing pay off in higher scores?

It depends. Students certainly need practice in writing to a prompt. They need practice in organizing their thoughts and drafting a piece in a limited amount of time. They need practice in writing under the same conditions they will find on the test.

But the bigger issue is this: How do I teach students to write well under time pressure and other constraints? The answer: By removing time pressure and other constraints. Remember, the best way you can prepare students for the test is to build fluency as writers, to help them become comfortable with the writing process as used for authentic writing.

Writing is a developmental process and cannot be learned out of sequence. Growing writers is a lot like growing flowers; you cannot hurry the blooms. It takes planting and watering and fertilizing and above all—time. If you want a student to learn how to write a piece effectively in 45 minutes, that student must first learn to write a piece with no time limits. In writing workshop, students learn that they write about the things they know about and care about. They feel free to start pieces and stop them, to develop them or throw them away. They get help from peers and from their teacher/writing coach. On some pieces, they develop editing and revision skills and eventually publish and share with a wider audience. They come to see how writers work and how they think. On those pieces they care about, they learn the writing process. And of course, they observe the writing process in short pieces they write as a class and in the work-in-progress that their teacher shares.

Students in this classroom have already learned the components of the writing process and have experienced the joy of writing. These students are ready now, in the weeks before the test, to learn about test writing. They are ready to see how they can compress the entire process they have experienced into an hour or less. Having examined the characteristics of good writing in the trade books they enjoy, they are now ready to see how a rubric that contains many of those same writing characteristics can help them evaluate the writing they do for the state test.

Or think of it in this way: If you can't buy a bicycle from the toy store and put it together in three hours, how would you like for someone to try to show you how to put it together in 45 minutes? Wouldn't it be better to take someone who already knew how to put a bike together and try to teach them to do it faster or with a different type of instruction manual?

The answer to the question about teaching to the test, obviously, is to do everything in its time. It's not wrong to teach to the test, as long as that teaching occurs in an atmosphere that honors writing (like the one described in Workshop 1) and occurs when young writers are already comfortable with writing.

Some of my colleagues use Power Writing[1] or teach a "five-paragraph essay" as the only approach to writing. They claim it raises test scores by giving students a framework for their writing and enhancing organization. Is that right?

Formula writing is like fad diets. If you need to lose 10 pounds to get into a new bathing suit for next week's pool party, the grapefruit diet or one of its cousins will probably work. Most likely you'll lose the weight and you'll fit into the suit and you'll look great and be happy.

You're also likely to gain those pounds back quickly.

No one doubts that fad diets—and formula writing—work in the short run. They just don't work long-term. Sometimes writing teachers who introduce formula writing to a class of low-achieving students score spectacular gains on writing achievement tests. Indeed, organization is one of the points on any rubric. Students are taught to pick out three points and put them in three paragraphs beginning with First, then Next, then Last. As an organizational technique, it does indeed help students. And if it is taught as one technique, similar, say, to clustering or brainstorming or freewriting, it can be useful.

But despite the helpfulness of clustering, brainstorming, or freewriting, nobody suggests that all writers should use those techniques before they begin to write. Not so with formula approaches. In some classrooms, they are taught as a destination, not a pathway.

And what about the test-success of those teachers who use them? Formula approaches are most useful in boosting the scores of non-fluent writers, whose work might jump a score point. But the formula approaches will only take writers so far. If the writing is scored on a 6-point scale, a formula approach might raise a class from a 2 to a 3 because the writing does indeed show an organizational structure. But the same cookie-cutter approach will also *prevent* those scores from going higher because the writing samples are obviously poured from the same mold. You certainly won't find the formulas in the "real world" of good writing. Look at magazines, newspapers, books—you probably won't find one example of the type of formula writing being taught in many classrooms.

The selling point of formula writing is organization, one of the most difficult skills to master for writers of any age. But the cure is worse than the disease. If you use formula approaches, treat them as techniques, rather than standards of good writing. For instance, you might show children how to use anecdotes as leads—but you would not want to suggest that all stories should begin with anecdotes. If you use Power Writing or another formula approach, teach it as one way to identify major points and to achieve focus. And then move on, showing students other ways to organize their writing. Review Workshop 5 for ideas on teaching effective organization in both narrative and expository pieces.

Many of my students bring limited experiences and little knowledge of the content of various areas of the curriculum. What if they have to write on something outside their background or cultural experience, something they have no knowledge of? How can I help them be better prepared?

First of all, students who have gaps in their content knowledge and experiences need to develop fluency as writers by writing every day. As their fluency develops, they are better able to draw upon and write about what they *do* know. But building their writing fluency is not enough. They will be more successful as writers through interaction with a wide variety of reading material, informational as well as literary. Teachers use writing models from literature to provide the bridge for these students from their experience to the world around them. Building the type of classroom writing environment discussed in Workshop 1 is even more important for these students than for mainstream student populations.

Field trips or classroom projects also provide valuable opportunities for students to write about direct experiences. Whether the springboard is a piece of literature or a hands-on activity, it is important that the teacher support these students through talking with them about their activities and ideas to help them move from thought to speech to writing. Helping students to verbalize— allowing them to explain or tell orally before writing—helps to clarify their thinking and improve their understanding of new material. It also gives valuable insight into their thought processes, insight that can be used to plan instruction.

And remember, the people who write the prompts for state writing assessments typically take into consideration the wide range of students who will be taking the test. Responsible test construction requires that topics be screened for bias of any type, including reasonable expectations for a broad population of children to have some knowledge or experience with a topic.

Should I simulate test conditions for my class? How long before the test should I start? How often should I do this?

Simulating test conditions may help your writers to know what to expect when the test is administered and to be more comfortable during the test. The simulation should provide students an opportunity to experience all the conditions of test day—including the test facsimile, time frame, room to be used, grouping of students, and test administrator.

There is no single answer to the question about how long before the test and how often you should simulate test conditions. Your knowledge of your students should be your guide. Consider the length of time they usually need to adapt to new experiences and their comfort level as writers, as well as the tradeoff you will make in using writing instruction time to practice for the test. This delicate balance is best achieved when students perceive that this is an opportunity for them to demonstrate what they know about writing effectively while under testing conditions.

Note

[1]   For an introduction to Power Writing that shows how it can be implemented in the classroom, see J. E. Sparks, *Write for Power*. Manhattan Beach, CA: Communications Associates, 1982.

AND SOME FINAL THOUGHTS

Writers and Writing Tests: The Bottom Line

❖ ❖ ❖ ❖ ❖ ❖ ❖

Countless hours are spent each year in American classrooms preparing for a state writing achievement test. Unfortunately, many of those are wasted hours. The premise of the book you are now finishing is that when we immerse students in great writing and spend time talking about how those authors crafted that writing—and then use those principles as we write in the classroom—students will be better prepared for writing tests.

Confident, fluent, experienced writers have the best chance of succeeding on any writing test. We can certainly give those writers an extra edge by previewing the type of test to be administered and practicing under the test conditions, but those advantages represent the frosting on the cake, not the main writing menu.

Writing is a developmental process. You can't take non-writers and rush them through to test success. As Robert White (1952) has said,

> [Parenting and teaching] can best be represented by the metaphor of raising plants. This should be encouraging, because raising plants is one of mankind's most successful activities. Perhaps the success comes from the fact that the husbandman does not try to thrust impossible patterns on his plants. He respects their peculiarities, tries to provide suitable conditions, protects them from the more serious kinds of injury—but he lets the plants do the growing. He does not poke at the seed in order to make it sprout more quickly, nor does he seize the shoot when it breaks the ground and

try to pull open the first leaves by hand. Neither does he trim the leaves of different kinds of plants in order to have them all look alike. The attitude of the husbandman is appropriate in dealing with children. It is the children who must do the growing. (p. 363)

Visit any teacher's supply store and you'll find shelves of books that promise to help you prepare your class for the state writing achievement test. And some do offer some interesting, if overpriced, activities that can provide valuable practice for students who are already experienced writers. But all their lesson strategies and worksheets cannot guarantee success for students if your goal is more to help them score well on the test than to help them become confident and fluent writers.

Journalist Dorothy Parker, a famed writer and wit, was once asked if she had any rules that would help writers to write better.

"Oh, yes," Ms. Parker answered. "I have six." Notebooks were opened by her listeners and pens were poised to take down her wisdom.

"Read, read, read, and write, write, write," she said dramatically.

It wasn't the answer her audience was looking for, but it was the right answer.

It still is.

Reference

White, R. W. (1952). *Lives in progress.* New York: Dryden.

APPENDIX

States Use Various Approaches to Assess Writing

Scott Beesley

❖ ❖ ❖ ❖ ❖ ❖ ❖

Most states now assess student writing. And though reliance on norm-referenced tests and criterion-referenced tests is widespread, there is also a growing understanding that these tests alone cannot measure students' ability to apply the knowledge gained from the mastery of education standards in real-life situations.

Therefore, the use of what has been termed *performance-based*, *authentic,* or *non-traditional* assessment has slowly gained momentum across the curriculum, especially in writing. In performance-based writing assessment, students demonstrate their writing ability by actually producing a writing sample—a definitive contrast to responding to multi-choice items about writing on a standardized test.

Assessment Formats: A Quick Analysis

Norm-referenced testing is essentially effective for establishing where your students are in reference to other students of the same general age or grade level taking the same test.

Criterion-referenced testing assesses students' mastery of specified standards in the state curriculum. Instead of comparing students with other students, performance is measured against state standards.

A performance assessment measures students' ability to actually apply knowledge in a more tangible way. Instead of responding to questions about a particular standard, students demonstrate their knowledge of the standard by doing something with it.

Or look at it this way: Picture 10 sailboats in a trans-Atlantic race. Norm referenced testing will tell you where each sailboat is in

> comparison to the other boats. Criterion-referenced testing tells you
> how far each sailboat has managed to sail. Performance-based as-
> sessment would assess each sailor's skills in actually sailing the boat.

The bottom line on writing assessment: Performance-based assessment measures a student's *ability to write*. Traditional assessment measures the student's *knowledge about writing*.

The use of writing samples in state writing assessments has
proliferated since the 1970s. Today, 42 states include writing samples
as part of their statewide assessment programs, while six of the
remaining seven states have tests in various stages of development.
(See Figure A.1.) Arizona and California have previously used writ-

State Writing Assessments Grades 1–8

State	Norm Referenced Test: Grades Administered	Criterion Referenced Test: Grades Administered	Performance Writing Assessment: Grades Administered
Alabama	3–8		5, 7
Alaska	4, 8		5, 7
Arizona*	3–8		
Arkansas	5, 7		
California*	4, 8		
Colorado	3, 4		4, 7
Connecticut		4, 6, 8	4, 6, 8
Delaware		3, 5, 8	3, 5, 8
Florida		4, 5, 8	4, 8
Georgia	3, 5		3, 5, 8
Hawaii	3, 6, 8	3, 5, 8	3, 5, 8
Idaho	3–8		4, 8
Illinois	3, 4, 6, 7	3, 5, 8	3, 5, 8
Indiana	3, 6, 8		3, 6, 8
Iowa			
Kansas		3, 4, 5, 6, 7	5, 8
Kentucky**	3, 6	4 or 5, 7 or 8	4, 7
Louisiana	4, 6	3, 5, 8	3, 5, 8

Figure A.1

Maine	4, 8, 11		4, 8
Maryland		3, 5, 8	3, 5, 8
Massachusetts**		4, 8	4, 8
Michigan		4, 5, 7, 8	5, 8, 11
Minnesota		3, 5, 8	5
Mississippi*	4–9		
Missouri	5, 8		5, 8
Montana*	4, 8		
Nebraska*	4, 8		
Nevada	4, 8		8.00
New Hampshire		3, 6, 10	3, 6, 10
New Jersey		4, 8	4
New Mexico**	4, 6, 8		4, 6, 8
New York		3, 5, 6	5, 8 (8th voluntary)
North Carolina	5, 8	3–8	4, 7
North Dakota*	3, 6, 8, 11		
Ohio		4, 6	4, 6
Oklahoma	3, 7	5, 8	5, 8
Oregon		3,5,8	3, 5, 8
Pennsylvania		5, 8	6 (mandated for 1/3 of schools)
Rhode Island	4, 8	4, 8	4, 8
South Carolina	4, 5, 7	3, 6, 8	6, 8
South Dakota	2, 4, 8		5
Tennessee	2–8		4, 8
Texas		3–8	4, 8
Utah	5, 8	1–6	District option
Vermont**		4, 6, 8	5, 8
Virginia	3, 5, 8		3, 5, 8
Washington	4, 8	4, 7	4, 7
West Virginia	3–11	4, 7	4, 7
Wisconsin	4, 8		4, 8
Wyoming	3–11	4, 8	4, 8

* Denotes states with performance based writing assessments currently under development
** Denotes states that use portfolios as the basis for writing assessment.

Figure A.1 (continued)

ing samples, but these were suspended while their state testing pro-grams were revised. Both states will be re-implementing writing samples with their new state assessments. States developing writing assessments using writing samples include Arkansas, Mississippi, Montana, Nebraska, and North Dakota. Only Iowa does not have a state writing assessment currently under development.

To obtain a writing sample, students in 38 states write in response to a prompt, which may come in the form of a picture, a brief scenario, or a combination of the two. The actual time given to write varies from a single session of 45 minutes to more than three hours over a three-day period. All samples are scored using rubrics, which also vary in number and complexity from state to state. Some writing samples are graded within the state by trained teacher-assessors, while others are shipped to various testing companies that develop the tests. Students in Kentucky, Massachusetts, New Mexico, and Vermont utilize writing samples selected from student portfolios.

According to Laura Barrett (1997), executive director of FairTest[1], "High quality assessment systems seek to measure and support critical thinking, creativity and the ability to use knowledge in real-life situations" (FairTest Press Release). While utilization of performance-based writing samples is a step forward in assessment of the student's ability to use knowledge in real-life situations, some cautions need to be raised:

1. Writing assessment becomes an exercise in responding to prompts, thus greatly reducing the authenticity of the writing situation.

2. The purposes of state assessments can conflict with each other. According to the *Report of the Assessment Programs in the United States* (1996), the three top purposes for state assessments are the improvement of instruction and curriculum, program evaluation, and monitoring school performance. In a growing number of states, student accountability—graduation examinations—has become a fourth purpose for statewide assessment. Combinations of purposes for testing create many tensions, especially in states that try to gauge both student and school accountability and instructional improvement. The report explains:

> Assessment for high-stakes accountability purposes typically requires standardization of content, administration, and scoring. . . . Test security is high with results determined at a centralized scoring center and returned weeks, sometimes months, after the assessment is administered. For an assessment to be effec-

tive as an instructional improvement tool, the results
need to be made available almost immediately so that
teachers can adjust their instruction . . . and modify
instructional strategies within the classroom. (p. 5)

The exception to that dominant scenario is writing samples
taken from portfolios, because teachers have had opportunities to
discuss and evaluate the student's writing. However, writing assessments based on prompts are a different matter. Because of the
time needed to assess the samples, and because teachers do not re-
ceive the writing samples back, prompt-driven assessments have
little value as tools for instructional improvement for individual students—this is still best achieved by ongoing assessment of student
writing in the classroom.

In 42 states, writing is assessed through a multiple assessment
approach that combines both writing samples and norm-referenced
and/or criterion-referenced tests. But whatever the approach—or
combination of approaches—writing assessment continues to be con-
troversial, as teachers, parents, legislators, and the public at large
search for and disagree over the best ways to measure writing development and the effectiveness of writing instruction.

Notes

1   FairTest is a national advocacy organization specializing in evalu-
     ation of standardized testing.

References

A status report of the assessment programs in the United States. (May
     1996). Report No. SSAP-AR-96. Washington, D.C.: North Cen-
     tral Regional Educational Education Laboratory.
*New state-by-state survey concludes most assessment systems need
     major changes; states just "tinkering at the edges of reform."* (Au-
     gust 1997). Fair Test press release. Available at http://fairtest.org/
     pr/tstkdspr.htm.

Author Index

❖　❖　❖　❖　❖　❖　❖

A

Atwell, Nancie, 17, 19
Avery, Carol, 10–13

B

Bagert, Brod, ix, 55, 57
Bartlett, Laura, 74
Baylor, Byrd, 39, 43
Beesley, Scott, 71
Biesty, Stephen, 40
Bradbury, Ray, 24, 26
Braddock, R., 12, 14

C

Calkins, Lucy, 25, 26
Clark, Roy Peter, 12, 14
Cleary, Beverly, 10, 37, 43
Crafton, Linda, 3, 14

E

Emig, Janet, 1, 14

F

Fox, Mem, 6, 14

G

Gardiner, John Reynolds, 21
Graves, Donald, 4, 8, 40, 44, 44

H

Houston, Gloria, 39, 44

K

Kilcup, Rick, 22–23

L

LaCoste, P., xiii
Lowry, Lois, 10, 21

M

Martin, Bill, 6, 14, 23, 41, 44

P

Parker, Dorothy, 70
Paulsen, Gary, 10, 22
Peck, Robert Newton, 48, 49

R

Robinson, Kathy, 6–7
Romano, Tom, 4, 14
Ross, Bob, 5
Routman, Regie, 11, 14, 52, 57

S

Sampson, Michael, viii
Schwartz, David, 40, 44
Scieszka, John, 37, 44
Shaughnessy, Susan, 8, 14
Sparks, J.E., 68
Spinelli, Jerry, 9, 14

T

Thomason, Tommy, 11, 14

W

Wallace, Bill, 22–23
Welty, Eudora, 55
White, Robert, 69, 70
Whitehead, R., 22, 26

Y

Yolen, Jane, 55, 57

SUBJECT INDEX

❖ ❖ ❖ ❖ ❖ ❖ ❖

A

Authenticity in writing, 16–17, 74

B

Bookbags, 6–7
Brainstorming, 42, 66, 67

C

Clustering, 39, 42, 66, 67
Conferencing, 8, 10–11
Craft lessons, 23–25, 26
Criterion-referenced tests, 71, 72

D

Demystifying writing, 5
Descriptive writing, 54, 56
Dialogue, 49

E

Editing, 8, 19
Elaboration, 45–49
Expository writing, 35–36, 40–44

F

FairTest, 74, 75
Five paragraph essay, 66
Florida Writes, xii, 7, 28, 35, 43, 59
Freewriting, 66, 67
Fluency 8, 15–19, 53

G

Grammar, 11–12, 32, 33, 34
Guided writing, 53–53

H

Hawaii Writing Assessment, xiii

I

Independent writing, 53
Interior monologue, 49

J

Journals, 8

K

Kid-Friendly Rubric, 32–34

L

Lead writing, 54

M

Marination in great literature, 6–7, 22, 53
Modeled writing, 52
Modeling, 3–5

N

Narrative vs. story, 43
Narrative writing, 35–40
Norm-referenced tests, 71

O

Off-topic writing, 55–56

P

Parent forums, 59–60
Performance-based assessment, 71–72
Poetry, 55
Power Writing, 21, 25, 66–67, 68
Publication, 8
Punctuation, 11
Pupil Evaluation Program (New York), xiii

R

Revision, 8
Risk-taking, 3
Rubrics, 27–34, 66, 74

S

Schemas, 36, 53
Shared writing, 52
Skills instruction, 11–12
Spelling, 11, 32, 33, 34

T

Teaching to the test, 65–66
Time to write, 7–9, 17

W

Webbing, 39, 42
Writing across the curriculum, 9
Writing workshop, 4, 8

About the Authors

❖ ❖ ❖ ❖ ❖ ❖ ❖

Tommy Thomason is a former professional journalist who now teaches in the news-editorial sequence of the Department of Journalism at Texas Christian University in Fort Worth. He also brings the perspective of a professional writer into elementary school classrooms, where he conducts writing workshops with children every week. Dr. Thomason is also author of *More Than a Writing Teacher: How to Become a Teacher Who Writes* and *Writer to Writer: How to Conference Young Authors*.

Carol York is a former elementary classroom teacher who taught students in grades one through six and Title I Reading. Her experience also includes service as supervisor of Title I Evaluation and Title I Reading. Ms. York is currently an elementary language arts supervisor for the School District of Hillsborough County in Tampa, Florida.

Scott Beesley, who wrote the appendix, is an associate professor of education at Grand Canyon University in Phoenix, Arizona. A former fourth grade teacher in Texas, Dr. Beesley has conducted research on the effect of grouping for reading and vocabulary instruction in first grade classrooms. He also founded an on-site elementary prescriptive reading program for at-risk students in Phoenix. He has produced two children's music tapes and travels nationally as a clinician and children's musician.

Scott Beesley, who wrote the appendix, is an associate professor of education at Grand Canyon University in Phoenix, Arizona. A former fourth grade teacher in Texas, Dr. Beesley has conducted research on the effect of grouping for reading and vocabulary instruction in first grade classrooms. He also founded an on-site elementary pre-scriptive reading program for at-risk students in Phoenix. He has produced two children's music tapes and travels nationally as a clinician and children's musician.